George W. Bible

Great European Conflict

Franco-Prussian War

George W. Bible

Great European Conflict

Franco-Prussian War

ISBN/EAN: 9783337170592

Printed in Europe, USA, Canada, Australia, Japan

Cover: Foto ©ninafisch / pixelio.de

More available books at **www.hansebooks.com**

GREAT EUROPEAN CONFLICT.

FRANCO-PRUSSIAN WAR.

CHASSEPOT-RIFLE vs. ZUNDNADELGEWEHR,

OR THE

NEEDLE GUN.

REAL CAUSE OF THE STRUGGLE.

NAME, TITLE, AND YEAR OF ACCESSION OF THE RULERS OF
THE EUROPEAN STATES.—KINDS OF GOVERNMENTS.—
ARMAMENTS, MILITARY AND NAVAL.

RHENISH PROVINCES.—STRATEGIC POINTS.

COMPILED AND ARRANGED FROM THE LATEST EUROPEAN OFFICIAL
SOURCES AND STATISTICS.

BY

G. W. BIBLE.

NEW YORK:
BIBLE BROTHERS, 432 BROOME STREET.
1870.

Entered according to Act of Congress in the year 1870,
By GEO. W. BIBLE,
In the office of the Librarian of Congress, at
WASHINGTON.

PREFACE.

The masses of this country possess very little reliable information of the real condition, character, and resources of the different European governments—especially those of France and Prussia.

This fact will be readily conceded by those who base their opinion upon extensive inquiry and observation. Indeed, there are comparatively few who are thoroughly acquainted with European facts and figures, except those of foreign birth, members of the press, officers of the government, and those whose peculiar bent has induced them to investigate.

In time of peace this lack of information is scarcely felt; but in time of war, especially a war like the present, there is a universal demand for all information relating not only to the war itself, but also to the politics and history of Europe.

To meet this demand, the author has collected the most important facts relating to France, Prussia, and other European powers, and arranged them in convenient shape for reference.

A twofold object has been kept in view in the preparation of this work, viz., to give facts which will enable all to judge understandingly of the causes of the present war, its probable results, the present situation of Europe, and, at the same time, present facts of interest concisely and impartially.

In a work of this kind, freely interspersed with quotations, it would be next to impossible to credit each item to its author; and it is hoped, therefore, that a general acknowledgment, with especial tender of thanks to *attachés* of the European consulates, members of the press, and others, will suffice.

With the above explanation, this volume is respectfully submitted to the public.

CONTENTS.

	PAGE
GERMAN FATHERLAND. National Song	10
FRENCH MARSELLAISE. National Hymn	12
FRANCO-PRUSSIAN WAR	13
CASUS BELLI	14
NAPOLEON III.'S SPEECH TO THE FRENCH SENATE	14
NAPOLEON III.'S ADDRESS TO THE FRENCH PEOPLE	15
KING WILLIAM'S ADDRESS TO THE REICHSTAG	16
REAL CAUSE OF THE STRUGGLE	17

FRANCE AND PRUSSIA COMPARED.

POPULATION AND NUMERICAL STRENGTH OF THEIR ARMIES	17
"SINEWS OF WAR"	17
WAR MATERIAL AND QUALITY OF ARMS	19
FRENCH AND PRUSSIAN FLEETS	22
ZUNDNADELGEWEHR VS. ST. CHASSEPOT	24
ZUNDNADELGEWEHR OR NEEDLE GUN	25
CHASSEPOT	27

FRANCE.

PORTRAIT OF NAPOLEON III.—AREA—POPULATION—GEOGRAPHICAL POSITION—COAST LINES—CONTINENTAL BOUNDARIES—ADVANTAGEOUS MILITARY POSITION, ETC.	31
INTERNAL COMMUNICATION—CANALS, PUBLIC ROADS, AND RAILWAYS CONSTRUCTED WITH REFERENCE TO MILITARY MOVEMENTS IN TIME OF WAR	32, 33, 34
ROADS CONVERGING AT METZ	34
GOVERNMENT, ETC.	34
PORTRAIT OF OLLIVIER	
THE FRENCH ARMY 1867-'68-'69-'70	35, 38, 39
COMMANDERS OF CORPS D'ARMÉE	39

FRENCH MARSHALS, SERVICES, ETC.

MCMAHON, CANROBERT, BAZAINE, VAILLANT, FOREY, RANDON, CHANGARNIER, LE BŒUF, COUNT DE PALIKAO, ETC.	41, 42, 43, 44
FRENCH ZOUAVES	44
FRENCH NAVY	46
COMMANDERS OF FRENCH FLEET	48

PRUSSIA.

PORTRAIT OF KING WILLIAM I.—AREA—POPULATION—OLD PROVINCES—NEW TERRITORY ACQUIRED IN 1866	48
GOVERNMENT—CHAMBER OF DEPUTIES—PORTRAIT OF BISMARCK—KING WILLIAM I., CROWN PRINCE FREDERICK WILLIAM, PRINCE ROYAL FREDERICK CHARLES—PUBLIC REVENUE—PUBLIC DEBT, ETC.	49

CONTENTS.

	PAGE
PRUSSIAN (AND NORTH GERMAN) ARMY	49, 50
CORPS, HEAD-QUARTERS, AND COMMANDERS OF CORPS	51

GENERALS OF THE PRUSSIAN ARMY.

PRINCE FREDERICK CHARLES	51, 52, 53, 54
CHARLES BERNARD, BARON VON MOLTKE	55
ALBRECHT THEODORE EMIL VON ROON	56
CHARLES EBERHARD HERWARTH VON BITTENFELD	56, 57
CHARLES FREDERICK VON STEINMETZ	57, 58
NAVY—NAVAL COMMANDERS	58, 59
GREAT PRUSSIAN NAVAL STATION	59, 60

NORTH GERMAN CONFEDERATION.

STATES, AREA, POPULATION—RULERS—GOVERNMENTS, ETC.	61, 62
PARLIAMENT—FEDERAL CONSTITUTION	62
ARMY AND NAVY	62, 63

SOUTH GERMAN UNION.

STATES, AREA, POPULATION—REVENUE, PUBLIC DEBTS, RULERS, GOVERNMENTS, ETC.—MILITARY AND OTHER TREATIES WITH NORTH GERMAN CONFEDERATION	63
ARMY AND NAVY	64
BAVARIAN AND WURTEMBERG ARMIES	64
THE ZOLLVEREIN	64, 65

RIVERS OF FRANCE AND GERMANY.

RHINE	66, 67
MOSELLE, SARRE, MAIN, NECKAR, ETC.	68

RHENISH PROVINCES AND STRATEGIC POINTS.

RHENISH PROVINCES	69, 70, 71, 72
COBLENZ	72, 73
KREUZENACH	74, 75
CARLSRUHE—MAYENCE	75
THIONVILLE, MERZIG, ZIERCK, SAAR LOUIS, BOULAY, TREVES, LAUTERBOURG	76
SAARBRUCK, FORBACH, METZ, ST. AVOLD, LUXEMBOURG	77
BINGEN, WORMS, MANNHEIM, NEUBURG, LANDAU, ETC.	78

HOHENZOLLERNS.

FREDERICK WILLIAM (the Great Elector), FREDERICK I., FREDERICK WILLIAM I., FREDERICK II. (the Great), FREDERICK WILLIAM II., FREDERICK WILLIAM III., FREDERICK WILLIAM IV., KING WILLIAM I.	79, 80
LOUISA AND NAPOLEON I.	81, 82
DESCENDANTS OF LOUISA	82, 83

GERMANY.

STATES, AREA, POPULATION, POSITION—OLD GERMANIC CONFEDERATION, DISSOLUTION OF THE DIET, WAR OF 1866	83, 84
NORTH GERMAN CONFEDERATION, SOUTH GERMAN UNION—GERMAN NATIONAL POLITICAL UNITY	85, 86

CONTENTS.

EUROPEAN WARS OF THE CENTURY.

	PAGE
TRIPLE ALLIANCE AGAINST FRANCE	86, 87, 88
BATTLE OF MARENGO	88, 89
THE NEW COALITION	89, 90
BATTLE OF AUSTERLITZ	90, 91
NAVAL BATTLE OF TRAFALGAR	91, 92
PRUSSIA ARRAYED AGAINST FRANCE	92, 93
BATTLE OF JENA	93
THE RUSSIAN CAMPAIGN	93, 94
THE PENINSULAR CAMPAIGNS	94, 95
THE EXPEDITION TO RUSSIA	96, 97
OCCUPATION OF MOSCOW	97
REVERSES IN GERMANY	98
THE ALLIES IN PARIS	99
NAPOLEON'S RETURN FROM ELBA	100
PRELIMINARIES OF WATERLOO	101
THE BATTLE OF WATERLOO	102
THE PEACE OF PARIS	104
THE EASTERN QUESTION	104, 105
DANUBIAN CAMPAIGN	106
BEFORE THE CRIMEA	107
THE GERMAN CAMPAIGN	108
AUSTRIA AND THE HOUSE OF SAVOY	110
EUROPEAN ASPECT OF THE STRUGGLE	111
THE CAMPAIGN IN SARDINIA	112
THE VICTORIES OF JUNE	112, 113
THE PEACE OF VILLA FRANCA	114
THE SCHLESWIG-HOLSTEIN WAR	115
PRELIMINARIES OF SADOWA	116
THE SEVEN DAYS' WAR	117
THE PEACE OF NIKOLSBURG	118
TREATY OF PRAGUE	118

REVIEW OF THE BALANCE OF EUROPE.

BRITISH EMPIRE.

COUNTRIES, AREA, POPULATION, GOVERNMENT, PARLIAMENT, QUEEN VICTORIA, REVENUE, NATIONAL DEBT, ARMY, NAVY, ETC.	119

RUSSIA.

STATES, POSSESSIONS, AREA, POPULATION, GOVERNMENT, IMPERIAL COUNCIL, ALEXANDER II., GRAND DUKE ALEXANDER, PUBLIC REVENUE, PUBLIC DEBT, ARMY, NAVY, ETC.	122

AUSTRIA.

CIS-LEITHAN PROVINCES, TRANS-LEITHAN PROVINCES, AREA, BOUNDARIES, POPULATION, GOVERNMENT, PARLIAMENT, PROVINCIAL DIETS, PUBLIC REVENUE, PUBLIC DEBT, EMPEROR FRANCIS JOSEPH, VENETIA AND LOMBARDY, ARMY, NAVY, ARMY IN WAR OF 1866, CASUALTIES, ETC.	124

CONTENTS.

	PAGE
COMPROMISE BETWEEN HUNGARY AND AUSTRIA	127
NAVAL AND MILITARY FORTRESSES	130

SPAIN.

PROVINCES IN EUROPE, DEPENDENCIES, AREA, POPULATION, DEPARTMENTS, COMMUNES, GOVERNMENT, CORTES, DEPOSITION AND ABDICATION OF QUEEN ISABELLA, REGENCY, MARSHAL SERRANO, PUBLIC REVENUE, PUBLIC DEBT, ETC.................130, 131, 132
ARMY—GENERALS, ETC. 132
FORTIFIED PLACES. 133
NAVY—NAVAL CHANGES SINCE 1861, ETC. 133

BELGIUM.

PROVINCES, AREA, POPULATION, GOVERNMENT..................... 134
LEOPOLD II., COUNT PHILIP OF FLANDERS, PRINCESS MARIA OF HOHENZOLLERN SIGMARINGEN.. 134
REVENUE, PUBLIC DEBT... 134
ARMY AND NAVY...134, 135
BELGIAN COMMANDERS—LIEUT.-GEN. LAURENT, MATHIEU BRIALMONT. 135
LIEUT.-GEN. BARON PIERRE EMMANUEL FELIX CHAZEL............. 136

HOLLAND.

AREA, POPULATION, POSITION, PROVINCES, DEPENDENCIES.......... 136
GOVERNMENTS, STATES-GENERAL, KING WILLIAM III., REVENUE, PUBLIC DEBT, ARMY, NAVY... 137

LUXEMBURG.

GRAND DUCHY.. 137
BOUNDARIES, DISTRICTS, AREA, POPULATION, LUXEMBURG THE CAPITAL, GOVERNMENT, PRESENT RULER PRINCE HENRY, REVENUE, ARMY, ETC. 138

ITALY.

BOUNDARIES, AREA, POPULATION, PROVINCES TAKEN FROM AUSTRIA AND THE PAPAL STATES... 138
POLITICAL DIVISION, GOVERNMENT, PARLIAMENT, KING VICTOR EMMANUEL III., REVENUE, PUBLIC DEBT, MILITARY STRENGTH, SARDINIAN LAW OF CONSCRIPTION, NAVAL FORCES, ETC.....139, 140

SAN MARINO.

BOUNDARIES, AREA, POPULATION, GOVERNMENT, RULERS, REVENUE, ARMY, ETC.. 141

PONTIFICAL STATES.

BOUNDARIES, AREA, POPULATION, STATES, GOVERNMENT, PIUS IX., PAPAL REVENUE, PUBLIC DEBT, ARMY, ETC..................141, 142
DECREE OF PAPAL INFALLIBILITY....................................... 143

PORTUGAL.

AREA, POPULATION, BOUNDARIES, PROVINCES, COLONIES, GOVERNMENT, CORTES, KING LUIS I., REVENUE, PUBLIC DEBT, ARMY, NAVY, ETC...152, 153

CONTENTS.

LIECHTENSTEIN.
AREA, POPULATION, BOUNDARIES, PRINCE JOHANNES II., REVENUE, FAMILY OF LIECHTENSTEIN. ETC. 153

SWITZERLAND.
BOUNDARIES, AREA, POPULATION, CANTONS, GOVERNMENT, FEDERAL COUNCIL, COUNCIL OF STATE, NATIONAL COUNCIL, PRESIDENT OF THE REPUBLIC, REVENUE, ARMY, ETC. 154, 155

DENMARK.
AREA, POPULATION, BOUNDARIES, DEPENDENCIES, THE ELBE DUCHIES, GOVERNMENT, DIET, LANDETHING, FOLKETHING, KING CHRISTIAN IX., PRINCE FREDERICK, REVENUE, PUBLIC DEBT, ARMY, NAVY, ETC. 155, 156

NORWAY AND SWEDEN.
NORWAY—AREA, POPULATION, BOUNDARIES, PROVINCES, GOVERNMENT, STORTHING, LAGTHING, ODESTHING, REVENUE, PUBLIC DEBT, ARMY, ETC. 156, 157
SWEDEN—AREA, POPULATION, BOUNDARIES, PROVINCES, REVENUE, PUBLIC DEBT, ARMY, NAVY, ETC. KING CHARLES XV., KING OF NORWAY AND SWEDEN 157

TURKEY.
AREA, POSSESSIONS, POPULATION, SULTAN, GRAND VIZIER, GOVERNMENT, COUNCIL OF STATE, REVENUE, PUBLIC DEBT, ARMY, NAVY, STATES WHICH PAY ANNUAL TRIBUTE, ETC. 157, 158, 159

GLIMPSE IN THE FUTURE.
MOTIVES AND PROBABILITIES OF THE WAR—POLITICAL CONDITION OF FRANCE AND PRUSSIA—IDÉES NAPOLÉONIENNES AND GERMANY, ETC. 159, 160, 162

UNITED STATES NAVY.
NORTH ATLANTIC FLEET... 162
SOUTH ATLANTIC FLEET... 162
MEDITERRANEAN FLEET.. 162
PACIFIC FLEET.. 162
ASIATIC FLEET.. 163
ON SPECIAL SERVICE... 163

VESSELS AT THE VARIOUS NAVY YARDS.
PORTSMOUTH, N. H., NAVY YARD................................... 163
BOSTON NAVY YARD... 163
BROOKLYN NAVY YARD... 164
PHILADELPHIA NAVY YARD... 164
WASHINGTON NAVY YARD... 164
NAVAL FORCE AT DISPOSAL.. 164

OUR IMPORTS AND EXPORTS TO FRANCE AND GERMANY.
IMPORTS... 164, 165
ARTICLES OF IMPORT... 165
EXPORTS.. 166
ARTICLES OF EXPORT... 166
SHIPPING—VESSELS, TONNAGE, ETC................................. 167

THE GERMAN'S FATHERLAND.

DES DEUTSCHEN VATERLAND.

Where is the German's fatherland?
Is't Swabia? Is't the Prussian's land?
Is't where the grape glows on the Rhine?
Where sea-gulls skim the Baltic's brine?
O no! more great, more grand
Must be the German's fatherland!

Where is the German's fatherland?
Bavaria, or the Styrian's land?
Is't where the Marser's cattle graze?
Is it the Mark where forges blaze?
O no! more great, more grand
Must be the German's fatherland!

Where is the German's fatherland?
Westphalia? Pomerania's strand?
Is't where the sand wafts on the shore?
Is't where the Danube's surges roar?
O no! more great, more grand
Must be the German's fatherland!

Where is the German's fatherland?
Say how is named that mighty land!
Is't Tyrol? Where the Switzers dwell?
The land and people please me well.
O no! more great, more grand
Must be the German's fatherland!

Where is the German's fatherland?
Say how is named that mighty land!
Ah! Austria surely it must be,
In honors rich and victory.
O no! more great, more grand
Must be the German's fatherland!

THE GERMAN'S FATHERLAND.

Where is the German's fatherland?
Say how is named that mighty land?
Is it the gem which princely guile
Tore from the German crown erewhile!
O no! more great, more grand
Must be the German's fatherland!

Where is the German's fatherland!
Name me at length that mighty land!
"Where'er resounds the German tongue,
Where'er its hymns to God are sung."
Be this the land,
Brave German, this thy fatherland!

There is the German's fatherland,
Where oaths are sworn but by the hand,
Where faith and truth beam in the eyes,
And in the heart affection lies.
Be this the land,
Brave German, this thy fatherland!

There is the German's fatherland.
Where wrath the Southron's guile doth brand,
Where all are foes whose deeds offend,
Where every noble soul's a friend.
Be this the land,
All Germany shall be the land!

All Germany that land shall be,
Watch o'er it, God, and grant that we,
With German hearts, in deed and thought,
May love it truly as we ought.
Be this the land,
All Germany shall be the land!

THE CELEBRATED MARSEILLAISE HYMN.

Ye sons of France, awake to glory,
  Hark, hark what myriads bid you rise;
Your children, wives, and grandsires hoary,
  Behold their tears and hear their cries.
Shall hateful tyrants mischief breeding,
  With hireling hosts, a ruffian band,
  Affright and desolate the land,
While peace and liberty lie bleeding!
  To arms, to arms, ye brave!
  The avenging sword unsheath:
March on, march on, all hearts resolved
  On victory or death:
March on, march on, all hearts resolved
  On victory or death.

Now, now, the dangerous storm is rolling,
  Which treacherous kings confederate raise;
The dogs of war, let loose, are howling,
  And lo! our walls and cities blaze.
And shall we basely view the ruin,
  While lawless force, with guilty stride,
  Spreads desolation far and wide,
With crimes and blood his hands imbruing?
  To arms, etc.

With luxury and pride surrounded,
  The vile insatiate despots dare,
Their thirst of gold and power unbounded,
  To mete and vend the light and air.
Like beasts of burden would they load us;
  Like gods, would bid their slaves adore;
  But man is man and who is more?
Then shall they longer lash and goad us?
  To arms, etc.

O liberty! can man resign thee,
  Once having felt thy generous flame;
Can dungeons, bolts, and bars confine thee,
  Or whips thy noble spirit tame?
Too long the world has wept, bewailing,
  That falsehood's dagger tyrants wield;
  But freedom is our sword and shield,
And all their arts are unavailing.
  To arms, etc,

EMPEROR NAPOLEON III.

FRANCO-PRUSSIAN WAR.

The absorbing topic of the day, which is now deeply agitating the entire civilized world, is the great struggle between two of the leading nations of Europe—France and Prussia.

Speculations are innumerable as to the result of the contest between these two powerful combatants, and its probable effect upon the nations of Europe, and evince the vital interest which humanity and civilization have in the struggle.

So much has been written purely of conjectural character concerning the conflict which threatens to spread such terrible slaughter and devastation throughout the countries engaged, and which may probably end in involving the combined powers of Europe in a general war for supremacy, that in a work of this kind, which deals only in possibilities, or, rather, facts and statistics, probabilities would seem to be out of place; but there is safety in the assertion that the sovereigns likely to be most deeply affected by the results of the war are Napoleon III., the Sultan of Turkey, and the Pope of Rome; and that the future National Unity of Germany is involved.

The duration of the war is dependent upon the numerical strength of the powers engaged and their availability of the "sinews of war;" the interests involved; and the attitude of the other leading powers.

CASUS BELLI.

Among the many causes of the war which have been enumerated are: Marshal Prim's tender of the Spanish crown to Prince Leopold, of the royal house of Hohenzollern (which numbers in its family the King of Prussia, and is allied by marriage to most of the Sovereigns of Europe), and the refusal of Prussia to accede to the terms dictated by France for the withdrawal of his candidacy; the failure of the intrigue of the Empress Eugenie to marry her niece (the Duchess of Alba) to Prince Leopold; the reconstruction of the Rhenish frontier; and the fear on the part of France of the ultimate establishment of the German National Unity, and the consequent ascendency of Prussia, involving the destruction of the equilibrium of Europe—termed the "balance of power."

Napoleon III. in his speech to the Senate says:—

Messieurs,—I experience great satisfaction on the eve of my departure for the army in being able to thank you for the patriotic co-operation you have given my government. War is legitimate when it is made with the assent of the country and the approbation of its representatives. You are right in recalling the words of Montesquieu. The true author of a war is not he who declares, but he who renders it necessary. We have done all that depended on us to avoid it, and I may say that the entire nation in its irresistible force has dictated our resolutions. I confide to you, in parting, the empress, who will call you around her should circumstances require. She knows how to fill courageously the duty which the position imposes. I take with me my son. He will learn in the midst of the army how to serve his country. Resolved to pursue with energy the great mission confided to me, I have faith in the success of our arms, for I know that France is standing behind me, and that God protects us.

In his address to the French people of July 23d he says:—

FRENCHMEN.—There are in the life of a people solemn moments when the national honor, violently excited, presses itself irresistibly, rises above all other interests, and applies itself with the single purpose of directing the destinies of the nation. One of those decisive hours has now arrived for France. Prussia, to whom we have given evidence, during and since the war of 1866, of the most conciliatory disposition, has held our good will of no account, and has returned our forbearance by encroachments. She has aroused distrust in all quarters, in all quarters necessitating exaggerated armaments, and has made of Europe a camp where reign disquiet and fear of the morrow. A final moment has disclosed the instability of the international understanding, and shown the gravity of the situation. In the presence of her new pretensions Prussia was made to understand our claims. They were evaded and followed with contemptuous treatment. Our country manifested profound displeasure at this action, and quickly a war cry resounded from one end of France to the other.

There remains for us nothing but to confide our destinies to the chance of arms. We do not make war upon Germany, whose independence we respect. We pledge ourselves that the people composing the great Germanic nationality shall dispose freely of their destinies. As for us, we demand the establishment of a state of things guaranteeing our security and assuring the future. We wish to conquer a durable peace, based on the true interests of the people, and to assist in abolishing that precarious condition of things when all nations are forced to employ their resources in arming against each other.

The glorious flag of France, which we once more unfurl in the face of our challengers, is the same which has borne over Europe the civilizing ideas of our great revolution.

It represents the same principles; it will inspire the same devotion. Frenchmen, I go to place myself at the head of that valiant army, which is animated by love of country and devotion to duty. That army knows its worth, for it has seen victory follow its footsteps in the four quarters of the globe. I take with me my son. Despite his tender years he knows the duty his name imposes upon him, and he is proud to bear his part in the dangers of those who fight for our country. May God bless our efforts. A great people defending a just cause is invincible.

NAPOLEON.

King William I., on opening the session of the Reichstag, or North German Parliament, on July 20th, said:—

"He had no interest in the selection of the Prince of Hohenzollern for the Spanish throne, except that it might bring peace to a friendly people. It had nevertheless furnished the Emperor of the French with a pretext for war unknown to diplomacy, and, scorning peace, he had indulged in language to Germany which could only have been prompted by a miscalculation of her strength. Germany was powerful enough to resent such language and repel such violence. He said so in all reverence, knowing that the event was in God's hands. He had fully weighed the responsibility which rested on the man who drives into war and havoc two great and tranquil nations, yearning for peace and the enjoyment of the common blessings of Christian civilization and prosperity, and for contests more salutary than those of blood. Those who rule France have shrewdly studied the proper methods of hitting the sensitive pride of that great neighbor nation, and, to promote selfish interests, have misguided it."

"Then," concluded the king, "as our fathers before us have done, let us fight for our liberty and rights against the wrongs inflicted by a foreign conqueror; and as He was with our fathers, so God will be with us in a struggle, without which Europe can never enjoy lasting peace."

REAL CAUSE OF THE STRUGGLE.

The apparent causes of the war are too trivial to be seriously discussed. A misunderstanding about the Spanish succession, a hasty word from the King of Prussia, or a mere act of petulance by Louis Napoleon, could never precipitate a contest between two nations like France and Germany.

The possession of the Rhine frontier may be summed up as the true cause of the war. But this frontier carries with it the mastery of Central Europe. It belongs to Germany by right and by actual possession. It has been won by France repeatedly during the last two centuries, but it has always been wrested back from her grasp. But France sighs for the boundaries of the times of the Grand Monarch, Louis the Fourteenth, and the First Napoleon, and if the present French emperor can minister to the vanity of the people in this respect, he may safely reckon on transmitting his crown to his son. For Prussia, or rather for Germany, the loss of the Rhine frontier would be political ruin. The German people comprehend this fact, and they will resist the aggressions of France to the bitter end.

FRANCE AND PRUSSIA COMPARED.

POPULATION AND NUMERICAL STRENGTH OF THE ARMIES.

France has a population of thirty-eight millions. That of the North German Confederation, consisting of Prussia, with the annexed States of Hanover, Hesse-Cassel Schleswig-Holstein, Nassau, and Frankfort, and the German States north of the river Main, amounts to nearly thirty-one millions. The South German States, excluding Austria, number nine millions. Thus the balance in point of population is slightly in favor of Germany. The French navy, with its fifty-five iron-clads and their 1,032 guns, against the Prussian navy, with but four such vessels and their fifty guns, and similar disparity in other classes of war steamers, is indisputably superior. But although since the unexpected victory of Prussia in 1866 the efficiency of the French army as well as that of the French navy has been steadily increased, and the effective force of the army, with the reserve, has been brought up to eight hundred thousand, a number larger by two hundred and sixty-three thousand than it had at the commencement of the Crimean war, yet the Prussian army has also been steadily increased, until it contains six hundred and fifteen thousand, of whom four hundred and fifty thousand are in active service, while the reserve of Prussia, consisting of the entire male population of suitable age, will enable her to bring into the field, for a defensive campaign, a full million of thoroughly drilled soldiers. Thus, in a military point of view, France and the North German Confederacy seem to be not very unequally matched.

"SINEWS OF WAR."

The famous war-treasure of the King of Prussia amounts, with accumulated interest, to two hundred millions, and the government has about the same amount in its coffers. What renders the wealth of France great is its elasticity. There are thirteen hundred millions of specie now in the Bank of France. The Bank of France can advance five hundred millions to the government against an emission of treasury notes. Prussia can raise about a quarter of this sum. At the time of the Exhibition of 1867, a celebrated

English calculator drew up a table by which the respective wealth of nations could be seen at a glance, and an extract from it will not be without interest here.

By putting the finances of England at par—
France represented 86 per cent.
Holland represented 71 per cent.
Belgium represented 63 per cent.
Switzerland represented 47 per cent.
Bavaria represented 38 per cent.
Baden represented 32 per cent.
Prussia represented 17 per cent.

So that the wealth of France is to that of England as 86 is to 100; the wealth of France is to that of Prussia as 86 is to 17.

WAR MATERIAL AND QUALITY OF ARMS.

Let us place Prussia and France face to face. On this side of the Rhine and on the other, the number of men ready to enter in campaign is about equal. Prussia has her needle-gun—an excellent arm. France has her chassepot, and one tried at Mentana. Prussia has her field artillery and mitrailleuses, on which she very justly counts; but France too, has her mitrailleuses and her field artillery. For seven years has France steadily improved and perfected her famous mitrailleuses, and has multiplied them so that to-day there is not a battalion of infantry or sharp-shooters which has not at least two in its ranks. The Prussian arsenals are gorged. The French arsenals are full to overflowing. Since the campaign of 1866, Prussia has spent 110 millions in renewing and modernizing its war material, much of it, however, being used in the war crowned by Sadowa. France has spent 210 millions on her military stores—camping equipments, provisions, drugs, ambulances, in a word, all the accessories of the grand theater of war, have been stored in the Invalides and the Ecole Militaire.

The mitrailleuses themselves are not the latest thing out of the supreme refinement of the destroying art. The mitrailleuses only are known to the public, but it appears that France has better than this, although the public may not be aware of it. But a short time since people began to talk of engines of war, not yet named, of the *Commander C——— M———*. These, to believe the report of one who witnessed recent experiments with them, constitute something miraculous in destructive inventions. Their extreme range is 3,000 yards only, which is the mean range of the mitrailleuses, their elder sisters, but these new and formidable inventions surpass them in massacring power as much as the mitrailleuses themselves surpassed every thing which had preceded them. At 2,500 yards the effect of these engines, which have been temporarily baptized "*les filles du commandant C. M.*," is so terrible, so certain, that a single regiment could force its way with them through an army, sowing death and terror before it. But, the reader may say beyond the number and courage of the army, beyond the armament, beyond the engines of war, beyond stores, there is the question of the sinews of war—money, to which we have already adverted. The new mitrailleuse above referred to under the curious title of "*les filles du commandant C. M.*," is now creating immense curiosity in Europe. This arm was invented two years ago, and experiments with the first model were made with the greatest secrecy at Vincennes and Mendon. To prevent spies obtaining information, or getting a glimpse of the gun, or rather mitrailleuse, a cordon of troops surrounded the place where the experiments were being carried on, out of view of the inventor and the gentlemen forming the commission appointed by the emperor to test the merits of the arm, with orders to allow no one to pass. The arm when approved was manufactured in the Vosges, the same surveillance and caution being observed. As soon as the guns were ready they were packed in boxes, which were sealed and sent to the various arsenals. No instructions were given in its use until the eve of the war, when four men in each regiment were conducted secretly to a convenient spot and taught how to maneuver it. A gentleman employed on the commission above referred to states that all he would vouchsafe to divulge on the subject of the arm is that it is on the Gatlin principle of small caliber, and is used to repel cavalry charges and attacks in column. Like mountain howitzers it has no carriage, and is carried by two men, who hold it when fired, there being little or no recoil. This arm must not be confounded with the ordinary mitrailleuse or Gatlin gun, which is mounted on a carriage, nor must it be supposed that it possesses equal powers of destruction. While the former can be used by placing it on the sides of a square, or at intervals along a column, to repel cavalry or an advance in columns, the latter can be used as a field battery, and with deadly effect. The range too, of the two engines of war is different. The sphinx has only a range, as will have been observed, of 3,000 yards, while the mitrailleuse *proprement dite* can be used at from 4,500 to 5,000 yards. To give an idea, however, of the deadly execution of the new mitrailleuse we cite the result of experiments made with it at Satory a short time back. Three hundred old cavalry horses were packed in a field at a distance of 1,200 metres from the gun, and three minutes after the order had been given to "turn the coffee-mill" not one remained standing. The next day the experiment was repeated under better auspices, as the gunner had been drilled to perfection in the use of the arm. Five hundred horses were this time operated on, and in ninety seconds they were lying dead on the field.

The truth is that as an engine of war in any thing approaching a general action the Prussian mitrailleuse is considered by the Germans as practically useless. This prejudice enables the gentlemen of the *rive droite* to turn up their noses a the French adaptation of Gatlin's system.

THE FRENCH AND PRUSSIAN FLEETS COMPARED.

The iron-clad squadron of Prussia comprises the celebrated King William, the Prince William, the Prince Carl, and the Prince Adalbert: the first-named is the most formidable iron-clad afloat except the Hercules; the two next are first-class iron-clads, and the last is a powerful, swift little armor-clad gun-boat, carrying two very heavy guns of Krupp's steel. The King William deserves more than a passing notice. She was designed by Mr. Reed, and built at the Thames Ironworks for the Turkish government. When she was finished the sultan could not afford to pay for her, so she was offered at the same price to the then Board of Admiralty, who declined to buy her, and Prussia at once came forward and offered £30,000 more. When Prussia had got her, the English Board of Admiralty saw their mistake, and tried to outbid Prussia, but it was then too late. This vessel has a speed of 14 knots, carries 8-inch armor, and has 28 guns—four 100-pounders and twenty-four 300-pounders. The King William is, in fact, not a vessel, but a little fleet in herself. Being very long, she is not handy or very easy to turn, and is therefore liable to the danger of being "rammed." If she can avoid this she would be an overmatch for four Continental iron-clads. The King William is the flag-ship. Four French vessels of the Flandre's class would have quite enough to do to take the King William alone, to say nothing of her two powerful consorts and the armored gun-boat. In the Baltic the Prussian squadron will join with six other Prussian gun-boats, all of which are heavily armored, carrying two of Krupp's monstrous guns, and have a high rate of speed. The other vessels of the Prussian navy are wooden frigates and corvettes, which would be of small account as cruisers, and could never attempt to keep the sea.

The French have now on their list of iron-clads 51 vessels; 45 of these are finished and at sea; 6 are building, and not likely to be finished within the next two years. Of these vessels, no fewer than 36 are wooden vessels, razeed, and plated with armor; only 11 are built entirely of iron; only 1, the Marengo, is composite, with a frame of iron, and sides of wood coated with armor. The most costly French-built vessel is the Couronne, which cost for hull and fittings, £191,000. The most costly in the whole fleet, is the Rochambeau (late Dunderberg), which the French bought from the United States in 1867, paying £480,000 for her. With the Dunderberg came also the Onondaga, which was cheap at £80,000. The three most formidable vessels which the French have ever planned, are the Colbert, Trident, and Richelieu, which were begun last December at Toulon. The first two are sister ships of 8,314 tons, 320 feet long, coated with 8-inch armor, and intended at present to carry 30 ponderous guns. The Richelieu is to be of the same length and armor, but of 7,180 tons. These vessels will be larger than any iron-clads ever yet projected. The Victorieuse, another great iron-clad of more than 4,000 tons, figures in the French list, but this has only been ordered, and not yet begun. La Gallissonière, too, is very backward in its progress, and will take more than another year to finish.

Of the French fleet, 11 are under 1,200 tons, 14 under 3,000, and 14 over 3,000 but under 5,000. Taking the mean average of the speed of all on trial trips, it gives scarcely 10 knots the highest, the Marengo giving only 14.5, and some as low as 7 knots. The average armor plating of the French vessels is $5\frac{1}{2}$ inches, ranging from 4 inches to $8\frac{1}{2}$ inches. The thickest armor, however, is a mere belt above and below the water line, and none of the French vessels have the powerful armored bulkhead across the stem and stern to save them from the raking fire, under which they would fall easy victims to an active enemy. The greatest weight of armor which the largest class of French vessels carry is 1,800 tons, and the smallest, 279 tons, and their greatest number of guns is 14.

ZUNDNADELGEWEHR vs. ST. CHASSEPOT.

VIRGIL was right in supposing that some place was due to "arms" in his famous ballad. "Arms and the man," he sang; but had he known what an arm of precision it was, or could he have hoped to use the *zundnadelgewehr* in a hexameter, the praises of Æneas would have been sounded less, and dactylic measures would have indicated the rapidity of the chassepot—the chassepot which "did wonders at Mentana." Some attention is due, in the study of modern warfare, to these weapons, seeing that it is on their use and merit that victory may depend.

Providence, that was on the side of the heaviest battalions in the days of the first Napoleon, is on that of the arm of precision and rapidity in those of Frederick William and the third Bonaparte. This was the story and the moral of the late Prusso-Austrian war. It was taught and read on the field of Sadowa, and Custozza had been a Sadowa, if the Italian allies of Prussia had had the Prussian weapon. It was the story of the Italian war where rifled cannon mowed down the Austrian white coats. It was the moral of Mentana, where Garibaldians afforded a satisfactory target and a rational test for the French chassepot. It was a knowledge of the superiority of the Prussian weapon that kept France back when the black eagle swooped down and carried crowns to its aerie, and tore the title-deeds of Central Europe into shreds. In truth, Providence is on the side of the army that has a weapon which in rapidity makes one man equal to six, and in accuracy each of these six almost equal to half a score. This is a scientific and hardly a muscular age, and the providence of the Little Corporal's conceit is to-day a scientific providence which despises a Croat or a Cossack, and has a mighty reverence for a snider or a chassepot.

In this new war the chassepot and the Prussian breech-loader will be fairly tried against each other. But each foe brings into the fight new weapons which will complete the test. There is the French mitrailleuse, which, it is said, can rain bullets like hail; there is also the Prussian *kugelspitzen*, which showers conical shot. Whether hail or conical shot will carry the day it is impossible to say; but it is noticeable that the war of the nineteenth century is transferred to the artisan's shop, and that diplomacy and " tented fields " are but agencies and instruments wherewith is obtained a trial of the inventive genius of bellicose nations.

THE ZUNDNADELGEWEHR OR THE NEEDLE-GUN.

The Prussian needle-gun is the invention of Mr. Dreyse, a manufacturer of arms at Sommerda, who spent over thirty years in trying to construct a perfect breech-loading rifle. The cartridge is inserted at the rear, and the ignition is produced by the intrusion of a needle into the fulminate attached to the cartridge. The barrel is 36.06 inches long, and is rifled with four grooves down to the breech, where the chamber, or bed for the cartridge, is smooth and a little larger than the bore. The bed enlarges slightly to the rear so as to admit the cartridge freely, and the lower part of the bore for a distance of 6.17 inches is enlarged so that the ball is gradually compressed into grooves. The rear of the barrel is conical, and is called the mouth-piece. Over this part there is a six-sided cylinder, which holds all the mechanism of the piece. The air-chamber, next to the cylinder, has the needle pipe screwed into its breech.

The gun is loaded in this way: After it has been brought to a nearly horizontal position, with the butt resting on the right hip, and the left hand at the lower band, and the chamber drawn back from the mouthpiece, the cartridge is inserted through the opening in the cylinder into its place, the chamber again brought up to the mouth-piece by means of the handle, and turned to the right. The locket is shoved up, and the notch of the mainspring engages the catch at the inner rear end of the chamber. At the same time the middle offset of the needle-bolt is pressed against the trigger-stop, thus compressing the spiral spring.

Now let the trigger-stop be drawn down by pressure on the trigger so as to clear the offset of the needle-bolt. The bolt will dart forward from the effect of the spring, and will strike the square end of the needle-pipe, which projects sufficiently to pass through the powder of the charge and inflame the fulminate.

At the time of the adoption of this new gun the cartridge was altered, the sabot being enlarged and placed between the powder and the ball.

The ball is spherio-conical. The charge of powder is 56 grains. The weight of the Prussian needle-gun is 10.27 pounds to 11.3. The mechanism can be taken apart without screw-driver, vise, etc. It can be safely and easily cleaned, and the gun being small, is particularly adapted for use in the contracted space of loop-holes, on horseback, etc. The objections to the Prussian needle-gun are the danger of a weakening of the spiral spring and the possibility that the needle may not be propelled with sufficient force to pierce the cartridge. On account of the ease and rapidity with which it is loaded, there is also danger of a waste of ammunition, as the soldier, in the heat of battle, will often fire his piece as fast as possible, even when he knows the firing has no effect. To make the best use of the needle-gun the soldier requires special training. The Prussian army is very well trained to its use, and in this respect has an advantage over the French, who have never been into a great battle with their chassepot.

The range of the needle-gun is from 1,400 to 2,000 yards.

The gun is never loaded or reloaded while at "aim," simply because it is impossible to do so.

The powder is not ignited at the rear end of the cartridge, but next to the ball, where the igniting matter is placed in a kind of socket of papier mache; and this is what gives more power to the ball, the powder burning from the front to the rear.

The cartridge is made up—ball in front, ball socket with igniting matter and powder. The shape of the ball resembles that of a cucumber, and is called long lead (*lang blei*).

The recoil of the gun is only felt when it becomes very much heated, and the air chambers are filled with the refuse of powder. When clean no recoil is felt at all.

In case the needle should break, or bend, or otherwise become useless, a new one can be inserted in less than five seconds. Each soldier carries an extra supply of about six needles.

The Prussian army has but one caliber for all small-arms, so that infantry, or sharp-shooters can be supplied with cartridges from any cavalry pistol or carbine cartridge wagon.

THE CHASSEPOT.

The fire-arm which has been adopted by the French army is the celebrated chassepot rifle, which is probably the most efficient weapon ever put into the hands of an army of infantry. It resembles the Prussian needle-gun, but possesses several improvements. During the late war between Prussia and Austria, the effective work of the newly invented needle-gun attracted the notice of all fighting nations, and the French, anticipating that they would some time be called upon to fight Prussia, immediately set to work to invent a weapon that should surpass the needle-gun in its power as an engine of war. The result was the invention by M. Chassepot, after long and careful study, having the Prussian gun to aid him and to improve upon. After the new rifle had been tested over and over again, the attention of the emperor was invited to it, and it was not long before he was convinced of its superiority, and ordered its adoption in the army.

One of the principal improvements which the chassepot has over the needle-gun of Prussia is, that its movement is simpler, and instead of being tightly inclosed in the breach by a cylinder, it is almost fully exposed, and the employment of india-rubber as an obturator. It is said that the Prussian gun, after it has been discharged several times in quick succession, becomes hot and damp in the chamber, owing to the inability of the gas, which comes back after the explosion of the cartridge, to escape. The inside soon becomes dirty, and the soldier is required to take his piece apart and clean it. The French gun is always open, and while there is no gas shut up in the chamber to corrode the metal, it can in a moment be cleansed from dirt or rust, and the soldier is always able to quickly discover any accident to his rifle.

An opening on the right-hand side of the chamber is for the insertion of the cartridge. This chamber is filled by a movable cylinder, which may be moved back or forward by the handle; a cylinder surrounds the shaft and a car revolves around the ram. It contains the spring by which the needle is propelled. The rear-end of the shaft is made in the shape of a handle; the spring is compressed when the handle is drawn back. The shoulder on the shaft comes in contact with the cylinder when the arm is at rest.

When loaded and ready for firing, the two parts are drawn asunder. The shaft also serves to protect the needle, which is surrounded by the same, and is forced out of the front end of the shaft as soon as the trigger is pulled. After the cartridge has been inserted the knob is pressed forward, and is then laid over to the right-hand side. The aperture is now closed. By the first of these two movements the cylinder is moved forward, thereby forcing the cartridge into the breech; the second movement secures the cylinder, so that it can be thrown back by the force of the explosion. The pulling the trigger releases the spiral spring, which then forces the needle through the percussion wafer.

It is claimed that this gun is not so easily clogged as the Prussian needle-gun, and is more substantially built.

The chassepot is handled in the following manner: While loading, hold the gun in the left hand, with the butt-end resting on the left hip. The lever is then turned with but one movement, from right to left, and with another pulled back, after which the cartridge is inserted into the opening thus effected. By a third movement—pushing back the lever into its original position—the gun becomes ready to be fired off. The projectile is a rather long slug, with the end rounded and pointed like our rifle ball. The charge, which is attached to it in a paper covering, is composed of a peculiar powder, especially manufactured for the purpose. The distance at which this gun carries with certainty is very considerable—over 1,000 metres. Both the infantry and the chasseurs have only the one model, but the bayonets differ, in so far as those of the chasseurs are sword bayonets.

The troops sent to save Rome from the Garibaldian bands were armed with chassepots when they embarked, and exercised with them during the passage to Civita Vecchia. A brigade supported the Papal troops. The chassepot spoke for the first time at Mentana. Its effect was terrible, and the delighted commander of the French troops exclaimed, "*Le chassepot fait merveille.*" In Algeria the rapidity of firing and the range of the chassepot again did wonders. The powerful tribes Doni-Menia and Beni Ghuill were forced to submit within two days, although hitherto, surrounded by inundations and thick woods, they had occupied an impregnable position. There is little doubt that fear of the chassepot, and long, straight streets went far toward saving Paris from a revolution at the time of the late *plebiscite*. There is nothing new under the sun. Breech-loaders were actually proposed during the time of Napoleon I., and that emperor is said to have foreseen and understood the advantages which would accrue from their introduction some days before his death. In the Musée de l'Artillerie there is a revolving matchlock musket, and an arm, called *l'Amusette* of Maréchal Saxe. In the "Correspondence de Napoléon I.," is a letter from the Minister of Police to the emperor concerning a breech-loader, patented by Pauly, a gunmaker of Paris. Pauly received a gratuity of ten thousand francs, and his system was submitted to a military commission. It was rejected as being too complicated and unfit for a campaign. From respect for M. Pauly the commission kept silence and rejected the arm without publishing its defects. The idea of breech-loaders, however, was not abandoned, and in 1813–14, a manufactory was established at St. Etienne for the fabrication of guns and pistols *à la* Pauly. The result was not satisfactory.

FRANCE.

GEOGRAPHICAL POSITION.

FRANCE is bounded north by the German Ocean and Straits of Dover; northwest by the English Channel; west by the Atlantic Ocean, including that part of it called the Bay of Biscay; south by Spain and the Mediterranean Sea; east, by Italy (Sardinian States), Switzerland, and Baden; and northeast by Rhenish Bavaria, Rhenish Prussia, Luxembourg, and Belgium. It comprises an area of 203,241 square miles, divided into 86 *Departements*, which are subdivided into 363 *Arrondissements*, 2847 *Cantons*, and 36,843 *Communes*, with an aggregate population of 38,192,094.

COAST LINES.

The length of the coast line, without allowing for minor indentations, is, along the German Ocean and English Channel, 560 miles; along the Atlantic, 500 miles; and along the Mediterranean, 260 miles; amounting in the aggregate to 1,320 miles.

CONTINENTAL BOUNDARIES.

The continental boundaries are formed—on the southwest, by the Pyrenees, 250 miles; on the east, by the Alps, 155 miles, the Jura, 167 miles, and the Rhine, 100 miles; and on the northeast by an arbitrary line of about 290 miles.

ADVANTAGEOUS MILITARY POSITION.

On taking a survey of this great country, it is impossible not to be struck with the advantages which it derives from its position. It not only forms a continuous and compact whole, but though united to the Continent by a line of about 900 miles, is so much isolated from it by great natural boundaries, that the only direction in which it can be considered open to hostile attack is on the northeast, where a line of fortresses has made barriers almost as impenetrable as those barriers which, in other directions, have been provided by nature. ·On the north and west a long line of coast gives it immediate access to the great ocean thoroughfares, and by its harbors in the Mediterranean it exercises a commanding influence both in Africa and the East.

INTERNAL COMMUNICATION—CANALS, PUBLIC ROADS, AND RAILROADS CONSTRUCTED, MORE FSPECIALLY WITH REFERENCE TO MILITARY MOVEMENTS IN TIME OF WAR.

Canals.

The canals of France are numerous, and their object has been to connect all the great river basins, and thus give a continuous water communication throughout the interior and from sea to sea.

Canal du Midi, or Canal of Languedoc, starting from a point on the Garonne, below Toulouse, is continued in an east-southeasterly direction into the Lagoon of Thau, and thereby gives a continuous water communication between the Atlantic and Mediterranean, in the line of the important towns of Bordeaux, Agen, Toulouse, Carcassonne, and Narbonne. Three separate canals cut across the basin of the Rhone: the Canal du Centre, or of Charollais, begins at Chalons-sur-Saône and proceeds to Digoin on the Loire; the Rhone and Rhine Canal, so called from uniting these two rivers, partly by the intervention of the Doubs; and the Canal of Burgundy which, proceeding also from the Saône, communicates with the Yonne, and through it to the Seine. The effect of these three canals is to break down the barriers which isolate the basins of the Rhone, Loire, Seine, and Rhine, and give navigable access from any one of them into the other three. The longest of all the canals is that which unites Nantes with Brest, the chief use of which is to keep open an important channel of communication in time of war, when it might otherwise be effectually closed by British cruisers. France possesses 86 canals, having an aggregate length of 2,350 miles.

Roads.

The public roads of France are classed as Great Roads (*Routes Royales*) and Department Roads. The former are 26 in number, having an aggregate length 24,900 miles; the latter 97 in number, with a length of 22,500 miles. Besides these, there are a great number of country or by-roads (*chemins vicinaux*) in all the departments, and especially in those on the frontier, adapted to the movements of armies.

Railways.

In the construction of railways, France is undoubtedly the foremost nation of Europe. Taking Paris as the center, a main trunk proceeds north to Amiens, where it divides into two branches, one of which proceeds north to the coast at Boulogne, and the other northeast past Lille into Belgium. A branch from Lille, turning west, ultimately throws off two branches, one proceeding to Calais and the other to Dunkirk.

Starting again from Paris, a line runs west-northwest, keeping close to the banks of the Seine, until it reaches Rouen, when it forks, sending one branch north to Dieppe, and the other west to Havre.

The termini of these roads are Dunkirk, Calais, Boulogne, Dieppe, and Havre. The next great trunk from Paris proceeds, with very little deviation, east to Strasbourg, and then almost due south through the left valley of the Rhine to Basel. Another trunk, extending south, forks soon after quitting Paris: one branch takes a southeast course first to Dijon, and thence to Chalons; the other

2*

branch continues south to Orleans. Here it again forks, and sends off two important lines, one south-southeast to Bourges and Nevers, and the other southwest to Tours. From Tours a branch goes west-southwest to Nantes, and another south for Bordeaux. From Bordeaux it extends along the Garonne, and nearly in line of the Canal du Midi to the Mediterranean. A line commences at Marseilles and proceeds circuitously northeast to Avignon, and from there almost due north to the Paris trunk line. A branch of the Marseilles line leaves it at Beaucaire and is carried west to Nimes, where it forks, sending a branch north to Alais, where the main line proceeds southwest past Montpellier to the port of Cette. These are the principal railway lines of France.

ROADS CONVERGING AT METZ.

The only roads leading from France into Prussia converge at Metz. One of these roads runs parallel with the line of the railroad to Luxembourg as far as the little town of Thionville, situated on the left bank of the Moselle, and heavily fortified. It then branches off in a northerly direction, passes through Sierck, another fortified town, situated on the Moselle, near the boundary line of Prussia and Belgium. Here it enters Prussia, striking Saarburg first, and next the town of Treves. Another road from Metz enters Germany near Saar-Louis, and proceeds from thence in an irregular line to Mayence. These two main roads are connected by numerous cross-roads, which offer ample ground for the maneuvering of armies.

GOVERNMENT.

Since 1789 France has changed its government more frequently than any civilized nation on the globe, having had fourteen different constitutions in sixty-five years. The first serious check to the old despotism was the assemblage of the States General in 1789 which framed a constitution embracing the idea of a limited monarchy. In 1793, it was succeeded by a purely democratic constitution, which was frequently changed between the years 1795 and 1799. In 1799 Napoleon was chosen First Consul, and under him France became an empire, 1804, and continued so, with various interruptions, until 1815, when the restoration of the Bourbons took place in the person of Louis XVIII.

The revolution of 1830 placed Louis Philippe on the throne. In 1848 another revolution occurred, which terminated in a republic, with the Presidency of Louis Napoleon. In 1851 Napoleon accomplished his famous COUP D'ÉTAT, supported by the army. He dissolved the House of Representatives, and proclaimed himself Emperor of France, under the title of Napoleon III., since which time the government has been administered with firmness and ability.

The government now is a limited monarchy, the legislative power being shared by the CORPS LEGISLATIF, which consists of two chambers.

REVENUE (budget of 1869), 1,995,404,666 francs.
PUBLIC DEBT (budget of 1868), 12,993,298,000 francs.

THE ARMY OF FRANCE.

The many reforms in the French army from the time it was considered invincible under the great chieftain, Napoleon I., up to the present dynasty, can not be the subject of this inquiry, which looks to recent events only, such as the reorganization in 1868 consequent upon Prussia's successful stroke against Austria and the establishment of the North German Confederation. The imperial government, desirous of maintaining the military rank heretofore occupied in Europe, thought necessary to frame a law which would enable it to wield an army of 800,000 men, ready in cases of emergency, to protect and march beyond the frontiers.

The law of February 1, 1868, respecting recruits for the army and the organization of the Garde Mobile, was intended to carry out this object. Its principal features are those of the law of 1832, but it increases the time of service to five years in the ranks and four years in the reserve. The military age is twenty-one; substitutes are allowed; measurement of the height is reduced by one centimetre, and the men of the reserve may contract marriage during the last three years of their service. A material alteration is the grouping of the different categories, there having been drawn formerly 23,000 of the first class, while the number at present is 63,000; the old system giving after a period of seven years, 161,000 experienced soldiers and 252,000 of only five months' drill, while with the present system, there are obtained 441,000 experienced and only 84,000 raw soldiers.

The real strength of the peace establishment of France, is about 400,000; to these must be added, in war footing :-

Nine categories of the second class at 12,000............	108,000
Four categories volunteers, or of those retaken from the reserve, at 7,000...................................	28,000
Four categories reserve first class at 60,000.............	240,000
Making a grand total of...............................	776,000

As the average cost of a soldier in France is 866 francs per annum, the war budget will amount to 672,000,000 and the peace budget to 346,000,000 francs.

Deducting from the above aggregate 80,000 for gendarmes, arsenals, powder manufactories, etc., 60,000 men for Algiers, and 65,000 men for 240 depots in the interior, there would be left for active operations at or beyond the frontier, a force of 580,000 men.

Of the 322,000 young men who annually attain the age of twenty years, 60,000 are taken for the Garde Mobile. This gives 300,000 men for five years. But owing to the abolition of many exemptions, the number will be increased

M. EMILE OLLIVIER.

in five years by 200,000; making a grand total of 500,000. The plan is to form 250 battalions of infantry of 1,600 men, and 125 batteries of 200 men—a force of no less than 425,000.

In order to provide for the cavalry, France in 1867 purchased 36,000 horses in Germany and Austria. Of these 14,000 were farmed out to agriculturists, who might work them, but are bound, when called upon, to return them in good condition within fourteen days.

The artillery branch, the pride of the First Napoleon, counts 169 batteries, with 1,014 guns. The mitrailleuse, or revolving ordnance, is said to possess less precision than the Gatlin gun, but to excel it in rapid fire. The whole number of ordnance manufactured by the government from 1852 to 1868, was 8,845 of both rifle and smooth bore. In the year 1868 the government manufactured 100,000,000 chassepot cartridges, and the same quantity was furnished by private industry.

The strength of the French army on the 1st of October, 1867, was computed at 650,498 men; of whom 40,000 were furloughed; 65,263 were in Algiers; and 226,466 reserve.

The official returns on the 1st of December, 1868, give the active force in the interior as 378,852; in Algiers, 64,531; in Italy, 5,328 men. The reserve of 198,546 and the Garde Mobile of 381,723 swell the total to 1,028,980. From the active force should be deducted, however, 114,430 men on furlough.

In April, 1869, Marshal Neil reported the strength of the army to the Senate as follows: Effective force on March 1, 330,000, with the requisite number of horses. In the event of a war footing it would require the purchase of 28,000 horses. No power in Europe could bring its forces into the field with the same facility. The whole number belonging to the ranks is 400,000, and with well-drilled reserves, 662,000.

The imperial decree of March 28, 1868, respecting the Garde Mobile has been followed by satisfactory results. The number of organized battalions was 142, batteries 91, and 2 pioneer bodies, and the force in future would amount to 2,000 battalions, representing a force of 550,000 men. On the 1st of October, 1869, the actual force was stated as follows:—

In the Interior	365,179
In Algiers	63,925
In the Papal Dominions	5,252
Total	434,356
The average number of furloughs was	108,831
Leaving actually in the ranks	325,525
The reserves amounted at the same time to	212,816
Total	647,172

An estimate of the strength which France could bring readily into the field, leaving the Garde Mobile out of the question:—

The field army, consisting of eight army corps or twenty-four divisions, is composed of 216,000 infantry, 27,000 cavalry, and 600 guns (not including twenty-four batteries of six mitrailleuses each), was estimated at 286,400 men.

Transport	286,400
The reserve, three army corps, nine divisions	93,600
Field troops remaining behind	50,000
Depots, fortresses, engineers	85,000
Total	515,000

To these should be added officers on leave, gendarmes, workmen, officials, etc., about 85,000, making a round number of 600,000.

In the second half of a year the above total would be increased by the annual levy.

THE ARMY ON PEACE AND WAR FOOTING, WITH NUMBER OF STAFF, MEN AND HORSES, AND REGIMENTS IN EACH BRANCH OF THE SERVICE, AND THE GENERALS COMMANDING THE DIFFERENT DISTRICTS IN 1870.

	PEACE FOOTING.		WAR FOOTING.	
	Men.	Horses.	Men.	Horses.
Staff	1,773	160	1,841	200
Infantry	252,652	324	515,937	450
Cavalry	62,798	48,143	100,221	65,000
Artillery	39,882	16,646	66,132	49,838
Engineers	7,486	884	15,443	1,400
Gendarmes	24,535	14,769	25,668	15,000
Troops of the Administration	15,066	5,442	33,365	12,000
Total	404,192	86,368	758,607	143,888

The infantry, in the above statement of the army on a peace-footing, comprises 124 regiments; the cavalry 66 regiments and one squadron, and the artillery 29 regiments. These forces are divided into what is known as the active army, the army of reserve, and the national guard. The active army, as enumerated, amounts to 404,192, the army of reserve to 400,000, and the national guard, when fully organized, to 538,723 men; making a total of 1,342,915 soldiers, over whom the following commanders exercise authority in their respective districts: Paris, Marshal Canrobert; Lille, Count l'Admirault; Nancy, Marshal Bazaine; Lyons, Count de Palikao; Tours, Count Baraguey d'Hilliers; Toulouse, General Goyon; Algiers, Marshal McMahon.

COMMANDERS OF THE CORPS D'ARMÉE.

There are eight army corps. Each army corps is composed of from three to four divisions of infantry, and from six to eight regiments of cavalry. Each division has three batteries of artillery, and one company of engineers, and comprises in its total force, from ten to twelve thousand men of all arms of the service.

The first *corps d'armée* is under the command of Marshal McMahon, duke de Magenta; the second corps is commanded by Frossard, General of Division; the third, by Marshal Bazaine; the fourth, by L'Admirault, General of Division; the 5th, by De Failly, General of Division; the sixth, by Marshal Canrobert; the seventh, by Felix Douay, General of Division.

The Major-General of the army is Marshal Lebœuf. The Assistant Major-Generals are Levren and Jarvas.

The Commander-in-Chief of the Artillery is General Soleille.

The Commander-in-Chief of the Engineers *Coffinières* is General De Noweck.

The Army of the Moselle, commanded by Marshal Bazaine, is composed of the second, third, and fourth corps, and has its several points of head-quarters at Saint Avold, Metz, and Thionville.

The general head-quarters of the French army is at Langres. The emperor assumes the chief command of the army, with Marshals Bazaine and McMahon as his subordinates.

The reserves are called "The Army of Paris."

The Army of the Rhine, under Marshal McMahon, is composed of the first, fifth, and seventh corps. Its head-quarter points are now at Strasbourg, Bitsche, and Belfort.

The corps under General De Failly, lying around Bitche, unites the two armies.

The army reserve is at the camp of Chalons-sur-Marne, under command of Marshal Canrobert. It is composed of troops of the line, re-enforced by reserves of every description which are called into the French service.

A battery of *mitrailleuses* (grapeshot cannon) is attached to each *corps d'armée*.

THE FRENCH MARSHALS—THE NATURE OF THEIR SERVICES— THE EVENTFUL PERIODS IN THEIR LIVES.

The African campaigns, which found the first field of active military duty for Marshals McMahon, Canrobert, Bazaine, Vaillant, Forey, Randon, Changarnier, Le Bœuf, and Count de Palikao, and followed the descent on Algiers by the French, were caused by an affront to the French minister. A new generation had arisen since the wars of the First Empire, and the young soldiers welcomed the field of adventure which Africa presented. The French occupation of Algiers met with little effective opposition from the Turks, but it aroused the fierce independent spirit of the native tribes, resulting, for a time, on the part of the French, in the shedding of rivers of blood and the spending of millions of treasure, without securing little more of the soil than their own garrisons. In 1831 the officers who are now the veterans of the French army, found themselves confronted by the daring chieftain, Abd-el-Kader, and for seventeen years this extraordinary man defended, with resolute bravery and masterly skill, his native land against the invaders. The nature of the campaigns in which the officers named, as well as others destined to be eminent before the close of hostilities, may be realized from some of the leading incidents. Marshal Chausel was sent, after some years of very indecisive fighting, with instructions to crush the Emir at one blow, who, on his part, fully alive to all that was going on, was not slow to meet his enemies. He promulgated the most terrible denunciations against all who should be found siding with the French, or supplying them with provisions; the consequence of which was that the French garrisons and outposts were almost starved, and could not obtain food except by foray, in which friend and foe were treated precisely alike. The Emir mustered upward of 50,000 men, and by his manœuvers succeeded in postponing the French advance until the wet season. It was not until November that the French arrived at Oran, on their march against Mascara. Mostacanem and Arzend were strongly garrisoned, and Chausel advanced into the enemy's country with 13,000 men. After several days of constant fighting, he succeeded in reaching Mascara, and avenged himself on Abd-el-Kader by reducing it to a heap of ruins. This wretched exploit achieved, the French were obliged to retreat again. They next took Tlemcen in January, 1836, and garrisoned it, and then returned to Oran. But although they defeated the Kabyles in a battle, the indefatigable Emir harassed their retreat, which they only effected after severe losses. This murderous and savage mode of warfare, which was no more than a system of forays, was without practical result to the French. As soon as the army had retired the inhabitants of Tlemcen rose upon the French garrison, their convoys were cut off, and General Arlanges, the second in command, was ordered to establish a fortified camp on the Tafna, for the purpose of covering Tlemcen and keeping open the communications between that post and the districts favorable to the French. In this advance he was attacked by the Emir and 10,000 Arabs, and driven back on his fortified camp, where he was shut up and compelled to remain until relieved by Bugeaud at the head of 4,000 men. Soon after, Bugeaud gained an important victory over the Emir, which for a time repressed his efforts against the invaders. In warfare like this, the present leading generals in the French army commenced their active military career. It was calculated to accustom them to the horrors of war, to make them equal to trying emergencies, and to render them capable of enduring all the fatigue attendant on fighting in a mountainous country, and under a burning sun.

The Crimean campaign next called to the field the veterans of the French army. The armies of the allies effected a landing at the Bay of Eupatoria, September 14, 1854. On their southward march toward Sebastopol they encountered the Russian forces, commanded by Prince Mentchikoff, on the banks of the Alma. A bloody battle was fought September 20, in which the Russians were compelled to retreat. On September 25, the British forces seized Balaklava, and on October 9, the regular siege of the the southern portion of Sebastopol commenced, the Russians having sunk vessels in the entrance to the harbor, and thus rendered the city unassailable by maritime force. On October 25, and November 5, the Russians vainly attempted to annihilate the besieging force in the battles of Balaklava and Inkermann, but afterward confined themselves mainly to the defense; their frequent sorties being intended more to harass and retard the siege than to relieve the place definitely. At Inkermann, where Canrobert won special distinction, the Russians lost in killed 3,011, and wounded 5,997; the English 462 killed, and 2,143 wounded; the French, 389 killed, and 1,337 wounded. Among the the sorties which marked the further progress of the siege, some assumed almost the character of regular field battles; for instance, an unsuccessful attack of the French upon a new redoubt; their first assault upon the Malakoff and Redan (June 18, 1855), and the battle of the Tchernaya (August 16), in which the Russians, numbering 50,000 infantry and 6,000 cavalry, made a last effort to break the aggressive force of the enemy. The trenches having been driven so near the Russian defensive works that another assault could be ventured, the final bombardment was opened September 5, and lasted for three days. On September 8, the Malakoff and Redan were stormed and taken by the allies after a desperate struggle, and the siege was virtually ended. In this campaign, the present leading French officers first engaged in war on a large scale, conducted with all the resources which the ablest engineers and inventors could afford, and demanding the most desperate valor in order to insure success.

The Italian war offered the French army employment on the historic field of Napoleon's campaigns. The first engagement with the Austrian forces was near Montebello, where their left wing was defeated. The allies being on the point of outflanking their right wing (battles of Palestro, May 31 and June 1), they recrossed the Ticino, and were routed in the great open battle of Magenta, June 4. Without risking a defense of the lines of the Odda and Oglio rivers, they retreated to the line of the Mincio. There, in the great battle of Solferino, they were defeated June 24, and peace soon followed. This was, with the exception of the Mexican campaign, in which Marshal Bazaine was conspicuous, the last conflict in which the French marshals had an opportunity of engaging in warfare on an extensive scale.

THE FRENCH ZOUAVES.—THEIR ORGANIZATION AND STYLE OF FIGHTING.

France possesses several special or extra corps entirely distinct from the regular army, the national guard, or the marines. One of them, and perhaps the most peculiar and eccentric, are the zouaves. There are two kinds of zouaves, the African, or original zouaves, who, in time of peace, are always stationed in Africa, and whose strength there is about 12,000 men, and the *zouaves imités*, or imitation zouaves, who are armed, equipped, and drilled like the original corps, but do not possess the same perfection in maneuvering, etc. These latter are only stationed a part of the time in Africa, the greater part they are stationed in various parts of France. In their armament the zouaves differ materially from the regular infantry, particularly in their bayonets, which have the shape of scythes, and their side-arm, which is the Algerian *yataghan*—that is, the peculiar short-sword of the Kabyles; also, in so far that they prefer to use their own private revolvers. No one can become a zouave who is not a born Frenchman, and a very large number of them are recruited among the Paris loafers and *gamins*. Their drilling comprises, besides the usual military evolutions, gymnastics; and no one can serve among them for any length of time who is not an accomplished and perfect swimmer, jumper, and climber. Their style of fighting differs accordingly from that of the regular infantry. They make no bayonet attacks in closed lines, but spread themselves out so as to have more room for striking about with their bayonet, and enter the enemy's lines on the full run with long bounds.

It is stated, that "one of their eccentricities, is their love for cats, and they prefer as pets the large gray and black cat of Algeria. The training of these cats is admirable. They know not only all the soldiers, but also their four-footed comrades belonging to the same battalion, and easily pick out their own masters under all circumstances. They are very obedient to them, and, not only on the march, but also in battle, take up their positions on their knapsacks—from which position they participate in the fight according to their own peculiar style, by jumping into the face of the enemy and scratching and biting in a furious manner. During the Crimean war, the wounds in the faces of the Russian soldiers from these cats were so serious and numerous that they had to establish at Odessa a separate ward in the hospital for the better healing of them.

"In climbing up and attacking a rocky height, the zouaves command their cats to the front to lead the way, and carefully watching the way the cats take, they follow them closely and take advantage of every foothold pointed out by their trusty and agile comrades."

NAVY.

The reorganization of the French navy was ordered by the government in 1855, and since that time France has paid special attention to its improvement. At the commencement of this year she had 62 iron-clads, 264 unarmored screw-steamers, 62 paddle steamers, and 113 sailing vessels. The following gives a statement of the number of vessels of each class, their horse-power, and armament, from official returns:—

CLASSES OF VESSELS.	No.	Horse-power.	Guns.
1. *Iron-clads:*—			
Ships of the line	2	1,800	62
Frigates	18	16,000	311
Corvettes	9	4,100	106
Coast guard ships	7	3,850	25
Floating batteries	15	2,010	146
Separate floating batteries	11	360	22
Total iron-clads	62	28,120	672
2. *Screw Steamers:*—			
Ships of the line	29	16,680	386
Frigates	24	10,100	574
Corvettes	21	7,940	156
Avisos	63	8,975	172
Gun-boats	78	1,871	95
Transports	47	10,222	160
Special boats	2	24	4
Total screw steamers	264	55,812	1,547
3. *Paddle Steamers:*—			
Frigates	11	3,450	32
Corvettes	7	1,870	18
Avisos	44	3,341	104
Total paddle steamers	62	8,665	154
4. *Sailing Vessels:*—			
Ships of the line	2	....	440
Frigates	11	....	57
Corvettes	7	....	25
Brigs	7	....	26
Transports	26	....	42
Smaller vessels	60	....	82
Total sailing vessels	113	....	672
Total War Navy	501	92,597	3,045

The largest iron-clad of the French navy is the Rochambeau, formerly called the Dunderberg, which was sold three years ago to the French Government for the sum of $2,000,000. The most remarkable among the other iron-clads are the Magenta, Solferino, Couronne, Normandie, Invincible, and the cupola-ship Taureau. The Magenta and Solferino were built on the same plan, and have wooden hulls, with plates varying from four to four and a half inches in thickness. Their armament consists of rifled breech-loading guns, 100-pounders, furnished with 155 rounds each.

The French navy is commanded by 2,218 officers of different grades. The sailors, afloat and on shore, numbered 39,346 in 1869, which, together with engineers, dockyard laborers, navy surgeons, and others connected with the force, bring the grand total of men engaged in the service of the imperial fleet up to 74,403. On the war footing the strength of the navy can be raised to 170,000 men, this being the number entered on the lists of the maritime conscription. Exclusive of the above are the marines and the colonial troops, amounting to 28,623 men.

The following is the list of the French iron fleet; those which have asterisks prefixed to their names are either just begun or have only been ordered:—

Ships' Names.	Tons.	Ships' Names.	Tons.
Magenta	6,737	Guyenne	5,711
Solferino	6,691	Héroïne	5,711
Friedland	7,180	Magnanime	5,711
Marengo	7,180	Provence	5,711
Ocean	7,180	Revanche	5,711
Suffern	7,180	Savoir	5,711
*Richelieu	7,180	Surveillante	5,711
*Colbert	8,314	Valeureuse	5,711
*Trident	8,314	Belliqueuse	3,347
Couronne	5,982	Alma	3,400
Gloire	5,630	Armide	3,400
Invincible	5,524	Atalante	3,400
Normandie	5,636	*La Galissonnière	3,400
Flandre	5,711	*Victorieuse	4,140
Gauloise	5,711	Montcalm	3,400

Ships' names.	Tons.	Ships' Names.	Tons.
Jeanne d'Arc	3,400	Saigon	1,507
Reine Blanche	3,400	Embuscade	1,222
Thetis	3,400	Impregnable	1,222
Taureau	2,438	Protectrice	1,222
Belier	3,400	Refuge	1,222
Boule Dogue	3,400	Arrogante	1,331
Cerbère	3,400	Implacable	1,331
*Tigre	3,400	Opiniâtre	1,333
Paixhans	1,539	Rochambeau (late Dunderberg)	7,000
Palestro	1,539	Onondaga (two-turret monitor)	2,000
Peiho	1,507		

THE COMMANDERS OF THE FRENCH FLEET.

Admiral De Lagraien commands the Rhine gun-boats, and Admiral Wellaumez the Northern Iron-clad Squadron of the French Navy.

PRUSSIA.

PRUSSIA comprises an area of 135,662 square miles, with a population of 24,043,296, and includes the following provinces or states:—

OLD PROVINCES.	Population.
Prussia	3,090,960
Posen	1,537,338
Brandenburg	2,719,775
Pomerania	1,445,635
Silesia	3,585,752
Saxony	2,067,066
Westphalia	1,707,726
Rhine Provinces	3,455,356
Hohenzetllern	64,632
Jade	1,748

NEW TERRITORY—ACQUIRED IN 1866.	
Hanover	1,937,637
Schleswig-Holstein	981,781
Cassel and Wiesbaden	1,379,745
Laurenburg	49,978
Garrisons outside of the kingdom	18,228
Total population	24,043,296

KING WILLIAM I.

Rhenish Prussia has the densest population.

Berlin, has a population of	702,432
Breslau,	171,926
Cologne,	125,172
Königsburg,	106,296

The government of Prussia is a limited hereditary monarchy, the legislative power being vested in the King and two Chambers of Deputies.

The present ruler, King William I., was born in 1797, and was the second son of Frederick William III. When his elder brother, King Frederick William IV. became insane, in 1858, William, then commander-in-chief of the Prussian army, was declared regent. His insane brother died in 1861, without issue, and the regent became king, under the title of William I. The great events of his reign thus far have been the annexation of the Elbe duchies and the important campaign which ended in the humiliation of Austria.

His queen, Augusta, is the daughter of the Grand Duke of Weimar.

The only son, and the heir to the throne, is the Crown Prince, Frederick William, who was born in 1831. Just before his father's elevation to the throne he married the eldest daughter of Queen Victoria.

The Prince Royal, Frederick Charles, the nephew of the king was born in 1828.

The Grand Duke of Baden, Prince Frederick, is a son-in-law of the King of Prussia, having married, in 1856, the Princess Louisa Mary, only daughter of that monarch.

PUBLIC REVENUE (according to budget for 1860) is 167,-536,944 thalers, and the public debt, 184,208,629 thalers.

PRUSSIAN (AND NORTH GERMAN) ARMY.

The army on peace footing comprises 319,358 men, and on war footing, 977,262 men; and consists of the guard and 12 army corps (the latter forms 6 divisions).

The (army corps of the) guard embraces 2 divisions of infantry of 2 brigades each, and one division of cavalry of 3 brigades. The 12 army corps have each 2 divisions, except the 11th, which has 3. Each division has two brigades of infantry and one brigade of cavalry. Altogether there are (inclusive of the guard) 13 army corps, 27 divisions, 54 brigades of infantry, and 28 of cavalry. The army of the kingdom of Saxony forms the 12th corps; that of Hesse-Darmstadt the 3d divisson of the 11th corps. Total force of the army is as follows:—

Classification.

Privates and Non-commissioned Officers.	Peace.	War.
Field troops	287,481	511,826
Depot do	....	180,672
Garrison do	13,046	265,082
Officers, Staff, and Military Schools	18,831	19,682
	319,358	977,262

The field army is composed as follows:—

	Peace.	War.
Infantry	200,312	371,680
Cavalry	54,005	46,137
Artillery	23,546	41,439
Pioneers	6,567	8,030
Train	3,051	44,540
	287,481	511,826

In time of peace the field army has 804 pieces of ordinance; in time of war, 1,272.

The above force comprises 118 regiments of infantry, 76 regiments of cavalry, 26 regiments of artillery, 13 battalions of engineers, and 13 battalions of trains.

As in the case of France, the military forces of Prussia and the North German Confederation may be said to embrace the whole adult male population, exclusive of all disabled by age or infirmity.

PRUSSIA. 51

The Prussian army is divided into eleven army corps, having the following commanders:—

Corps.	Head-Quarters.	Commanders.
1	Köningsberg	Gen. von Manteufel.
2	Stettin	Prince Fred. William.
3	Berlin	Prince Fred. Charles.
4	Magdeburg	Gen. von Alvensleben.
5	Posen	Gen. De Kirchbach.
6	Breslau	Gen. von Tumpling.
7	Munster	Gen. von Zastrow.
8	Coblenz	Lieut.-Gen. De Gobeen.
9	Schleswig	Lieut.-Gen. von Manstrein.
10	Hanover	Lieut.-Gen. von Voigts-Rhetz.
11	Cassel	Lieut.-Gen. von Plonski.

Commander-in-chief is KING WILLIAM I.

General Von Moltke is chief of staff of the Prussian forces.

The Prince Royal, Frederick William, commands the the left of the Prussian army, Prince Frederick Charles the center, and Herwarth von Bittenfeld the right.

The defenses of the coast are intrusted to General von Falkenstein.

The staff officers are the same as they were in the war against the Austrians in 1866.

THE GENERALS OF THE PRUSSIAN ARMY.

The leading general of the Prussian army is, in Prussia, regarded as far superior to the Crown Prince, and as the equal if not the superior of the veteran von Moltke.

Prince Frederick Charles of Prussia,

commander-in-chief of the Prussian army on the Rhine, son of Prince Frederick, was born March 20, 1828. He is the beloved Charles Alexander, and nephew of the king, and a man of such extraordinary military talents that he might be safely pronounced a military genius. The eyes of the entire German people are now turned upon him in unlimited trust and confidence. Like all

Prussian princes, Frederick Charles had to enter the Prussian army when scarcely ten years old, it being considered necessary that every descendant of the house of Hohenzollern, no matter what his individual inclination may be, should become fully acquainted with the military service of his country, and that, whatever career he may ultimately follow, he may be called upon at any moment to draw his sword for the defense of Fatherland in times of danger. With Frederick Charles, however, there was no need of compulsion. The warlike spirit of his ancestors animated him even in his earliest youth, and induced him to devote himself with enthusiasm to his military studies. The result of this innate love of everything connected with the army, soon became apparent in the rapid progress which he made in the military school of instruction. The study of the life and glorious deeds of Frederick the Great filled his leisure hours, and it is said that he was on several occasions severely reprimanded for passing entire nights over the history the "Seven Years' War" and the study of the plans of battle adopted by that illustrious captain. At the outbreak of the first war of Schleswig-Holstein in 1848, he was assigned to the staff of the commander-in-chief of the Prussian forces, General von Wrangel, when at the battle of Schleswig, his impetuosity and his entire disregard of all danger, while imperiling his life at every instant, did not fail to encourage the troops, and materially aided in securing the victory to the Prussian eagle. During the campaign in Baden in 1849, he likewise distinguished himself on various occasions. Fifteen years of peace now followed, during which the prince resumed his theoretical studies of the science of war, made himself familiar with all branches of the army, and showed conclusively his superior talent for the organization as well as for the skillful disposition of large armies. The disregard of treaties by Denmark, resulting in a declaration of war against that power by

Austria and Prussia, the second campaign in Schleswig-Holstein was soon entered upon, and although General von Wrangel was at first appointed commander-in-chief of the combined armies, the command of the Prussian division was intrusted to Prince Frederick Charles, December 15, 1863. He at once recognized the fortified place of Düppel, to be one of the greatest Danish strongholds, and a formidable barrier to the advance of the German armies into Danish territory. He therefore decided upon a regular siege and investment of the position. The severity of the winter in these northern latitudes interfered considerably with his operations, and it was not until April, 1864, that he thought safe to order first the bombardment and then the storming of the fortifications. Twice the assault was repulsed with serious slaughter, until at last the intrepid commander grasped the flag of the regiment of Royal Guards, and, personally leading his troops to a third attack, drove the enemy out of his stronghold and gained a decided victory, the Danes losing over 5,000 men and 118 pieces of artillery. Being defeated in several other important engagements, the Danes saw the impossibility of further resistance, and a treaty of peace was signed on October 30, 1864. At the outbreak of hostilities between Prussia and Austria in 1866, Prince Frederick Charles was called to the command of the first division of the Prussian army, immediately marched his troops to the frontier, which he crossed on June 23, and in ordering the attack upon the forces of the enemy, addressed his men with the words: "May your hearts beat toward God and your fists upon the enemy." A succession of splendid victories at Liebenau, Turnau, Podol, Münchengrätz, and Gitschin, having forced the enemy into the interior of Bohemia, Prince Frederick Charles, who knew the Austrians to have occupied a formidable position on the heights beyond the Bistritz, requested the crown prince, Frederick William, to come to his assistance with the second division of the army, but attacked the enemy on the morning of July 3d, without awaiting his arrival. The Prussians fought desperately; but the position of the enemy was so well chosen, and their artillery so favorably placed, that the prince could not gain a decided advantage over them, and it was not until the arrival of the second division, under the Crown Prince, that the enemy lost ground, retreated under the deadly fire of the Prussians, and was finally completely routed, running in all directions, and in the wildest confusion. This ended the celebrated battle of Sadowa. The enemy was pursued from the 5th to the 12th. Brün was taken, and the Prussian troops found themselves near the capital of Austria, ready, at a moment's notice, to march upon Vienna. The interference of France, resulting in the treaty of Prague, this ever-memorable campaign was at an end, Austria humiliated, and her former military prestige lost forever. As might be anticipated from a man who had taken such a conspicuous part in the brilliant achievements of the Prussian army, our hero, although proud of his troops, and willingly admitting their superiority over any European army which could then be marshaled against them, had nevertheless become aware of some serious drawbacks and errors hitherto overlooked in the organization of the Prussian army, and at once concluded to advocate such reforms as his experience had convinced him to be absolutely necessary. Meeting with opposition in high quarters, he is said to have resolved to submit his opinions to the approval of the highest military authorities, and it is generally believed that he is the author of an anonymous pamphlet published in Frankfort, which has attracted the greatest attention from the government, and has been the cause of the recent important reforms in the Prussian army.

It appears that the views expressed in this publication gained the approbation of the chief of staff, the renowned

Charles Bernhard, Baron von Moltke,
Born in Mecklenburg-Schwerin, October 26, 1800, who, after serving in the Danish army during his earlier youth, offered his services to the Prussian government, and was appointed second lieutenant in 1822. His superiority as a tactician and a strategist was soon fully appreciated, and ere long he was appointed to the general staff of the Prussian army. Here he found an extensive field for the rapid development of his extraordinary talents. In 1835 he was sent to Constantinople for the instruction and organization of the Turkish army, distinguished himself in the campaign of the Sultan against the Viceroy of Egypt, and returned to Prussia rich in honors and experience. He made rapid advances in the army, until he was definitely appointed chief of staff in September, 1858, in which position he has remained up to the present day, and has rendered such services in his reorganization of the Prussian army, the skillful planning of campaigns and all military operations, as can never be overestimated or too well appreciated. He took part in the war against Denmark in 1864, when he distinguished himself beyond precedent. About this time he published several works on military science, which have been translated into all modern languages, and have created for him a world-wide reputation. But the greatest field for the practical application of his genius, was offered to him during the campaign of 1866. It is said that, not only was he in constant possession of information about every movement of the army, but that he never was at a loss one single moment how to counteract all his adversaries' operations and turn them to his own advantage. His character is as firm as a rock, and, when once engaged in the planning of a military movement, nothing can detain him from carrying it out, as long as he feels morally convinced that he is in the right and there is a chance of success. In spite of his advanced years, he is said to be

still very robust, and has no fear of the fatigues of a campaign.

Albrecht Theodore Emil von Roon,

Minister of War and Marine, was born in the city of Colberg, April 30, 1803. He received his education in a Prussian military school, and was afterward assigned as a teacher to a similar institution in Berlin. Besides his assiduous studies of every thing connected directly with military science, he devoted himself especially to the publication of his now world-renowned topographical charts, and of works on history and geography. In 1831, he entered the Prussian army, and advanced step by step until he was appointed major-general in 1858, and shortly afterward Minister of War, in which position he applied himself diligently to the reorganization of the Prussian army. During the preparations for the campaign of 1866, he had occasion to prove to what point of perfection the process of mobilization had been carried in Prussia, and the number of troops, horses, and pieces of artillery, as well as the quantity of ammunition and provisions which could be sent forward to the theater of war at the shortest notice, are really astounding.

Charles Eberhard Herwarth von Bittenfeld,

General of Infantry and Commander of the Eighth Army Corps, born September 4, 1796, entered the Prussian army at the age of 15, fought at the battle of Leipsic, and took part in the invasion of France by the allies in 1814, where he served with distinction in several engagements and at the siege of Paris. During the second campaign in Schleswig-Holstein, in 1864, he achieved one of the most brilliant victories over the Danish army, and virtually brought the war to a close by taking possession of one of the most important positions of the enemy, the island of Alsen, and by almost annihilating the troops who were ordered to defend the place. The war of 1866 again called him into active service. He was assigned to the command of the Elbe army, and gave many proofs of his superior talent as a military leader and organizer. His participation in the battle of Sadowa was a glorious one, and his behavior on this and several preceding occasions was such, that he is now considered one of the bravest, most skillful and talented commanding officers in the Prussian army.

Charles Frederic von Steinmetz,

General of Infantry and Commander of the Fifth Army Corps, born December 27, 1796, was sent to the military school at Culm at the age of ten years, and soon showed a decided predilection for the army. He was a little over sixteen years old when he was ordered to Berlin and assigned to the corps of General York. Two years later he received his commission as lieutenant, was wounded at the battle of Dannigkow, fought with distinction at Königswartha, where a ball took away one of his fingers, while another wounded him severely in the thigh. But such was the ardor of his warlike temper that, although unable to walk, he insisted upon taking part in the battle at Bautzen, in May, 1813, on horseback. He fought in France in nearly all the engagements of 1814, and entered Paris with the armies of the allies. During the long term of peace which followed, he studied military science to great advantage, and after advancing rapidly to the rank of captain, he was soon after assigned to the staff. During the dispute between Austria and Prussia in 1850, on account of the Electorate of Hesse, Von Steinmetz was ordered to Cassel, and afterward appointed commandant of the place. Although it was his earnest desire to participate in the second campaign in Schleswig-Holstein in 1864, he was ordered elsewhere, and had to remain inactive against his will. During the campaign against Austria, Von Steinmetz commanded the Fifth Army Corps, and vanquished and dispersed three different Austrian army corps within the almost incredible short space of four days. Here it was that the Prussian cavalry, which had been hitherto considered inferior to the Austrian, or rather Hungarian horsemen, proved that they were not only their equals, but in many respects their superiors. His triumphant victory at Skalitz against forces of more than twice the numerical strength of the corps he commanded, procured for him the name of "the Lion of Skalitz." Throughout the entire campaign, Von Steinmetz did not meet with a single reverse, although he was often compelled to fight with the odds decidedly against him.

NAVY.*

Screw-Steamers,—Iron-clads,	Horse-power.	Guns.
Konig Wilhelm	1150	23
Prince Friedrich Karl	950	16
Kron-prinz	800	16
Arminius	300	4
Prince Adalbert	300	3
Hansa	450	8
Frigates and Corvettes,		
4 of 400 horse-power 6 guns each	1600	24
1 " 400 " 26 " "	400	26
2 " 400 " 14 " "	800	28
2 " 220 " 17 " "	440	34
Gun-boats,		
8 first-class of 80 horse-power 3 guns each	640	24
15 second-class 60 " 2 " "	900	30
1 Yacht	169	2
36 Corvettes	720	15
Total	9619	253
Sailing Vessels,		
3 Frigates		110
8 Brigs		40
3 Schooner-rigged vessels of 2 guns each		6
41 Gun-boats of 2 guns each		82
9 Gun-boats of 1 gun "		9
	9619	500

* The armament of Prussia (*per se*) is not given but in connection with the North-German Confederation.

The Prussian and North-German navy is manned by 2,471 seamen and boys, and officered by 1 admiral, 1 vice-admiral, 1 rear-admiral, 27 captains, 44 commanders, and 133 lieutenants. There are besides 5 companies of marines, 4 of infantry, and 3 of artillery, numbering 1,200 men.

The Prussian squadron is under Prince Adalbert, chief admiral.

GREAT PRUSSIAN NAVAL STATION.

There are three points of the greatest importance to Prussia to be defended along the Atlantic coast: the mouth of the Weser, with the opulent city of Bremen and its seaport—called Bremerhaven—which is situate about half-way between Bremen city and the mouth of the river and connected with the city by railroad; the wealthy city of Hamburg—the former queen of the Hansa—is situated west of the mouth of the river Elbe, and is up to this day the home of Germany's proudest merchant princes, who are the owners of great fleets of vessels; and the bay of Jahde is not far distant, with its naval station, which is destined by Prussia to become her principal marine harbor—in fact, a second Cherbourg.

This spot was originally, and as early as 1811, selected by Napoleon I. for a naval station, he being then in possession and controlling the whole of that part of the German coast, and he had it not only surveyed for that purpose, but he had already erected some fortifications when his downfall put an end to the scheme.

Prussia, without a suitable spot of her own, bought this same Jahde in 1854, on the strength of the old French surveys (the only ones then in existence), for the sum of 500,000 thalers from the Duchy of Oldenburg to which it then belonged. After thorough and exhausting surveys Prussia finally, about four years later (in 1858), commenced to build and fortify a marine harbor on the largest scale, and has ever since, and in spite of the greatest difficulties, pushed her work forward so that it is now very near completion.

The basins are large and capable of floating a fleet of the largest iron-clads. The fortifications are extensive, and the barracks already built and building will comfortably accommodate a respectable army. Two of the greatest drawbacks of this establishment are the want of good water, and the circumstance that the ebb tide falls fully twelve feet, thus preventing the largest sized men-of-war from entering the harbor at all except at high tide. The channel is also difficult, but that, in time of war, and as an additional means of defense, is rather desirable than otherwise.

COUNT VON OTTO BISMARCK.

NORTH GERMAN CONFEDERATION.

THIS CONFEDERATION WAS ESTABLISHED IN 1866, AND CONSISTS OF

PRUSSIA AND THE GERMAN STATES NORTH OF THE RIVER MAIN:

States.	Area.	Population.	Ruler.	Title.	Date of Accession.	Government.	No. Chambers
Prussia............	135,662	24,043,296	William I.	King	1861	Limited Mon.	2 Chambers
Mecklenburg-Schwerin....	4,701	560,618	Fred. Francis II.	Grand-duke	1842	" "	2 "
Saxe-Weimar.......	1,403	283,044	Chas. Alexander	Grand-duke	1853	" "	2 "
Mecklenburg-Strelitz..	997	98,770	Fred. William	Grand-duke	1860	" "	2 "
Saxony............	5,701	2,423,401	John	King	1854	Limited Mon.	2 Chambers
Oldenburg.........	2,470	315,622	Peter	Grand-duke	1852	" "	2 "
Brunswick.........	1,525	303,401	William	Duke	1831	" "	1 "
Saxe-Meiningen....	968	180,335	George II.	Duke	1866	" "	Sov. 1
Saxe-Altenburg....	491	141,426	Ernest	Duke	1853	" "	1
Saxe-Coburg-Gotha..	790	168,735	Ernest II.	Duke	1844	" "	1
Anhalt............	1,017	197,041	Leopold	Duke	1817	" "	1
Schwarzburg-Rudolstadt...	405	75,074	Albert	Prince	1835	" "	1 Chamber
Schwarzburg-Sondershausen	358	67,500	Fred. Gunther	Prince	1867	" "	1 "
Waldeck...........	455	58,805	George Victor	Prince	1852	" "	1 "
Reuss, Elder line	} 558	43,899	Henry XII.	Prince	1859	" "	1 "
Reuss, Younger line		88,097	Henry XIV.	Prince	1867	" "	1 "
Schaumburg-Lippe..	170	31,186	Adolphus	Prince	1860	" "	Mon. 1 Chamber
Lippe-Detmold.....	445	111,352	Leopold II.	Prince	1851	" "	1 "
Lubeck............	142	48,538	Dr. Roeck	Burgomaster	1863	Free City	
Bremen............	112	109,572	Dr. Duckwitz	Burgomaster	1863	Free City	
Hesse-Darmstadt (Up. prov.)		252,451	Louis III.	Grand-duke	1849	Limited Sov.	2 Chambers
Hamburg,..........	4,430	305,196	Dr. Seiveking.	Burgomaster	1865	Free City	
Total.........	162,790	29,907,359					

NORTH GERMAN CONFEDERATION.

PARLIAMENT AND FEDERAL CONSTITUTION.

The Parliament is composed of 296 deputies—one deputy for every 100,000 inhabitants.

The Federal Constitution of the North German Confederation assigns the presidency of the Confederation to the King of Prussia, who declares war, makes peace, concludes treaties, sends and receives embassadors in the name of the Confederation. (Chap. iv.)

The legislatures of Bavaria, Wurtemberg, and Baden, ratified the military zollverein treaties which their governments had concluded with Prussia; and at a convention of the South German States held in November, 1868, it was officially stated that the military conventions would be carried out, and that in case of war between Prussia and France, all the South German States would side with Prussia. It was also agreed, that early in 1868, the Customs Union Parliament should meet, composed of delegates from Southern as well as Northern Germany, thus giving to the German people, for the first time since 1848, a Parliament representing the whole Fatherland, with the exception of the German provinces of Austria.

ARMY AND NAVY.

The armament being computed in connection with that of Prussia, a distinctive statement of the respective numerical forces of each—from the data at hand—has been found inadmissible. The combined strength of both can be ascertained by reference to the article on Prussia, hence a repetition of the same is omitted here.

Extracts from the Federal Constitution relative to military service are, however, given, on which is founded an estimate of the effective army.

EXTRACTS FROM THE FEDERAL CONSTITUTION.

Every able-bodied male inhabitant serves in the active army from the age of 20 years to 27, and in the Landwehr till the age of 32.

The effective strength of the Federal Army for 10 years will be 1 per cent. of the whole population. (This would make the effective strength about 300,000 men.)

SOUTH GERMAN STATES.

The following comprise the South German States:—

States.	Area.	Population.	Revenue.	Public Debt.	Ruler.	Title.	Date of Access.
Bavaria*(deduct provinces ceded to Prussia).	170,688	7,774,464	Florins. 87,144,606	Florins. 334,405,150	Ludwig II.	King.	1864
Wurtemberg*	7,568	1,748,325	Florins. 22,395,981	Florins. 126,560,470	Charles I.	King.	1864
Hesse-Darmstadt † (except the upper province, which belongs to N. Germany).	2,970	564,465	Guilders. 9,407,008 Florins.	Florins. 2,088,000 Florins.	Louis III.	Grand-Duke.	1849
Baden †	5,912	1,429,199	28,598,998	3,228,003	Frederick.	Grand-Duke.	1832
	187,138	11,516,456					

* Limited Monarchy, two Chambers.   † Limited Sovereignty, two Chambers.

According to a conference held at Stuttgart, February 3, 1868, of the representatives of the four South German States for a discussion of a uniform militia organization, the following was agreed upon as the basis of further military arrangements:—

(Extracts) *Article* 2.—Military organization as largely as possible upon a system similar in principle to that of Prussia.

(Extracts) *Article* 3.—Standing army of the line and reserve to be about 2 per cent. of the whole population, 1 per cent. of which to constitute the actual effective force; and in no case to be lower than 1½ per cent. for the general strength of the standing army, and ¾ per cent. for the actual effective force. Time of service to commence after the 20th year; after 3 years' active service, to join war reserve of their division, with liability to be employed in time of war. After expiration of time of service in the standing army, to enter reserve battalions (first ban of the Landwehr); time of service in the standing army and in the reserve battalions (Landwehr) ends at the completion of the 32d year.

According to the above agreement the standing army of the four South German States would be 170,325 men, of which the full effective force would be 85.565 men.

BAVARIAN ARMY.

Peace footing—Officers, 2,139; officials, 742; men, 34,662; 8,647 horses and 192 guns. War footing—Officers and men, 69,064; reserve, 25,757; garrison troops, 22,614. Together with 17,236 horses and 240 guns.

ARMY OF WURTEMBERG.

The army in 1868 consisted of 34,405 men, of which 14,150 were in active service.

THE ZOLLVEREIN.

THE following stipulations were agreed to between the North German Confederation and the South German States in a conference held in Berlin, June 3, 1868:—

The treaties of the Zollverein concluded in 1865 to remain in force a period of twelve years.

The South German States to give up their power of veto; the Customs legislation henceforth belongs to the Federal

Council of the North German Confederation, to which the South German States will send thirteen plenipotentiaries in the following proportions: Bavaria, 6; Wurtemberg, 4; Baden, 3; and Hesse-Darmstadt 2. The South German States will also be represented in the Reichstag, to which it will send eighty-six deputies chosen according to the electoral law of the Confederation, as follows: by Bavaria, 48; Wurtemberg, 18; Baden, 14; Hesse-Darmstadt, 6. The proposals concerning the important modifications of the tariff of fundamental institutions of the Zollverein will be first discussed by the Federal Council. If there is a divergency of opinion the vote of Prussia will be decisive in the event of its being given for the maintenance of the existing dispositions. The States of the Zollverein abandon the privileges which some of them heretofore enjoyed. Those of the South German States which may consent to establish in their territories the tax on tobacco, which, according to the constitution of the North, will be established also in the Northern States, after the ratification of the preliminaries the general conference of the Zollverein, consisting of the representatives of Prussia, Bavaria, Wurtemberg, Baden, Saxony, Hesse-Darmstadt, and the States of Thuringen and Oldenburg, will assemble at Berlin to draw up on the bases put forward, the new treaty constituting the German Zollverein.

The preliminaries having been ratified by the South German States, the general conference assembled at Berlin on the 26th June, 1868, and, in accordance with provisions agreed upon, June 4th, drew up the new treaty constituting the German Zollverein, June 26th, which treaty received the sanction of all the South German Diets.

RIVERS OF FRANCE AND GERMANY.

THE RHINE.

THE Rhine, one of the most celebrated rivers of Europe, is formed in Switzerland by the union of two small streams, —the Hinter and Vorder Rhein. The Hinter springs from the glacier of Rheinwald, and the Vorder Rhein rises on the north side of Mount St. Gothard, at an altitude of 6,550 feet; these streams meet at Reichenau, in the canton of the Grisons.

The united stream flows generally north, past Mayenfeld, and enters the Lake of Constance on the southeast, near Rheineck; at Stein it quits the lake at its western extremity, flows west past Schaffhausen and Laufenburg, separating Switzerland from Bavaria. At Basel, where the Upper Rhine terminates, with an elevation of 755 feet, and a breadth of 550 feet, it turns to the north, and flows past Breisach and Strasbourg, Speyer and Mannheim, where its bed is 300 feet above the sea, between the territories of Baden on the east, and France and Rhenish Bavaria on the west. From Worms to Mentz it traverses the Hessian territory. At Mentz it receives the Main, and flows west to Bingen, where it turns to the northwest, passing Coblenz, Bonn, Cologne, and Dusseldorf, Wesel and Emmerick, below which it divides into two principal arms, the larger of which, called the Waal, or Wahal (ancient Vahalis), joins the Meuse (or Maas). The other, which still retains the name of Rhine, falls into the North Sea, in 52° 13′ north latitude. The principal affluents of the Rhine are, on the right, the Kinzig, Neckar, Main, Lahn, Ruhr, Lippe; and on the left, the Thur, Aar, Ill, and Moselle.

The total length of the Rhine, following its windings, is 960 miles, and its basin comprises an area of 65,280 square miles. Its breadth at Basel is 750 feet; between Strasbourg and Speyer 1,000 feet; at Mentz 1,500 to 1,700 feet; and at Schenckenschanz, where it enters the Netherlands, 2,150 feet. Its depth varies from five to twenty-eight feet, and at Dusseldorf fifty feet. The Rhine first becomes navigable at Chur (Coire), in the Grisons, but the navigation is not continuous until below Schaffhausen. From Strasbourg to Mentz, the burden of vessels is generally from 100 to 125 tons, from Mentz to Cologne 125 to 200, and from Cologne to Holland 300 to 450 tons. In the Netherlands it is connected by canals with its several branches and with the sea. The great North Canal unites it with the Meuse and the Nèthe, affluents of the Scheldt; and the Canal of the Rhone and Rhine in France connects it with the Rhone by the Saône, and a canal also connects it with the Seine. In Bavaria it communicates with the Danube by means of the Main and the Altmühl and Ludwigs Canal.

From Basel to Mentz it flows through a wide valley, bounded on the left by the Vosges, and on the right by the Black Forest and the mountains along the Bergstrasse. From Mentz the mountain ridges approach the stream at first only on the right bank, where they form the Rheingau; but at Bingen they begin to hem in the left bank also, and continue from thence to Königswanter to present a succession of lofty mountain summits, bold precipices, and wild romantic views. Pleasant towns and villages lie nestled at the base of lofty hills; above them, on all sides, rise rocky steeps and slopes, clothed with vines; and every now and then the castles and fastnesses of feudal times are seen frowning from precipices apparently inaccessible. At times the chain of ridges on either side opens out, and allows the eye to wander into romantic valleys, along which tributaries of greater or less magnitude dash down, or wind gradually to the parent stream.

The Rhine gives name to three circles of Baden, to a province of Hesse-Darmstadt, a province of Bavaria, two departments of France (Haut-Rhin and Bas Rhin), and a province of Prussia.

THE MOSELLE

Rises in the southeast department of Vosges, France, passes Remiremont, Epinal, Toul, Frouard, Pont-a-Mousson, Metz, and Thionville, in France; separates the duchy of Luxemburg from Rhenish Prussia, and joins the Rhine on the left of Coblenz. It is navigable from its confluence with the Meurthe near Frouard. The chief affluents in France are the Meurthe and Seille on the right, and in the Prussian States the Sarre on the right, and the Sure, Kyll, and Elz on the left. Its whole length is 328 miles.

RIVER SARRE

Rises in the Vosges Mountains, flows through the French departments of Meurthe and Moselle and a part of Rhenish Prussia, and joins the Moselle five miles southwest of Treves, after a north course of 120 miles, of which it is navigable for fifty miles.

THE MAIN.

The river Main rises by two streams, the Red and White Main, in the Fitchtelberg Mountains, North Bavaria, and flows very tortuously west, and joins the Rhine opposite Mentz. Its length is 280 miles. It is navigable from Regnitz (240 miles) to the Rhine. The chief affluents on the left are Regnitz and Tauber; on the right, the Saale.

THE NECKAR.

The river Neckar rises in the mountains of the Schwarzwald (Wurtemberg), on the frontier of Baden, flows generally north and west to Mannheim, where it joins the Rhine on the right. Length, 210 miles. It is shallow, and difficult of navigation. The chief affluent is the Jaxt, on the right.

RHENISH PROVINCES.

A GENERATION ago, Victor Hugo wrote a book on the Rhine, in which, besides giving the most fascinating and poetic of all descriptions of that famous stream, he cried out, "France, take back the Rhine," as he stood at the tomb of Hoche, who was buried on the shores of that river.

"Whose shall be the Rhine?" which is now being so terribly and fearfully contested for by the armies of France and Prussia, we give the translation of the poetical answer by Nikolaus Buker, entitled the "German Rhine," and the "French Reply," by Alfred de Musset, both perfect gems in their way.

GERMAN RHINE.

It never shall be France's,
    The free, the German Rhine,
Though raven-like she glances
    And croaks her foul design.

So long as calmly gliding
    It wears its mantle green,
So long as oar dividing
    Its mirrored wave is seen.

It never shall be France's,
    The free, the German Rhine,
So long as youth enhances
    His fervor with its wine.

So long as, sentry keeping,
    The rocks its margin stud;
So long as spires are steeping
    Their image in its flood.

It never shall be France's,
    The free, the German Rhine,
So long as festive dances
    Its lover-groups combine;

So long as angler bringeth
    Its lusty trout to shore,
So long as minstrel singeth
    Its praise from door to door.

It never shall be France's,
    The free, the German Rhine,
Until its broad expanse is
    Its last defender's shrine.

THE FRENCH REPLY.

Your German Rhine has been ours before!
   It has served our wassail bowls to fill.
Can singing its praise from door to door
   Efface the hoof-prints, legible still,
Of our cavalry charge that bathed its left bank in your gore?

Your German Rhine has been ours before!
   On its breast the wound yet gapeth wide,
Which conquering Condé made, when he tore
   Through its mantle of green to the farther side:
Where once the sire has ridden, shall the son not ride once more?

Your German Rhine has been ours before!
   Of your German virtues what remains
When across its flood our legions pour
   And the Empire over-clouds your plains?
When all your men have fallen, have ye other men in store?

Your German Rhine has been ours before!
   If ye your annals would fain forget
Your daughters remember the days of yore,
   And wish the Frenchmen among them yet,
For whom your vintage white they were always blithe to pour.

If your German Rhine be yours once more,
   Then wash your liveries in its tide;
But pitch your arrogance somewhat lower!
   Can ye recall with generous pride
Your myriad raven-beaks that drank the dying Eagle's gore?

May your German Rhine flow evermore
   In peace; and modestly may each spire
Be mirrored fair in its glassy floor!
   But oh! keep down your bacchanal fire
Which, else, may rouse to life again the victor hearts of yore.

The Rhine is, according to Frenchmen, the "natural boundary" of France. The Germans, however, do not agree with them. The people of the German Rhenish provinces are German in language, tastes, and feelings, and have no admiration for the French.

France owns the west bank of the Rhine from a few miles north of Basel, in Switzerland, to the frontier of the Palatinate at Lauterburg. The possession of the last-named district would add to the list of French cities, Spires, with its old cathedral, and the fortified places of Landau and Neustadt, besides a large number of smaller towns and villages. In Rhenish Prussia—speaking always of the western shore of the Rhine—the first town of importance is Worms, associated with the name of Luther. After passing over the flat, highly cultivated district through which the Rhine here sluggishly rolls along, the towers and bridges of Mayence loom in sight. This is a city of strategic and historic importance. Shortly further on is Bingen; and there begins the marvelous scenery which has given to the Rhine such world-wide celebrity, and has made familiar, the names of such trifling, though picturesque hamlets as Oberwessel, St. Goar, Boppart, Andernach, Bacharach, Remagen, and the like. Midway among these is Coblenz, overlooked by "Ehrenbreitstein's castled height," and still further down the stream is the collegiate town of Bonn.

The position of France in Europe is almost impregnable on all sides save one. From Calais, on the Straits of Dover, along her entire sea-coast boundary on the British Channel and the Atlantic Ocean, running north and west, her situation is admirable. On the south nature has also provided a boundary in the Pyrenees, which divides the empire from Spain and the Mediterranean Sea. From, say, Nice, she is bounded by the Alps, which separates her from Italy and Switzerland, to the Vosges Mountains, across thence to the Upper Rhine, and along that river to a point near the famous town of Lauterbourg. Here the boundary, which has been running east-northeast, abruptly turns to a north-northwest direction along an imaginary line, separating her from Bavaria, Rhenish Prussia, Luxemburg and Belgium.

It is this exposed frontier which is the cause of all the present difficulty. It has necessitated on the part of France and Germany the construction of a series of fortresses, of which the most formidable, are Strasbourg and Metz, in the first-named country, and Mayence, Ehrenbreitstein (opposite Coblenz), and Cologne in Prussia.

Having the Rhenish-German provinces west of the Rhine, the Grand-Duchy of Luxemburg and the Kingdom of Holland, France could look with complacency upon the growth of Prussia, for she would then possess a natural frontier, made by the Rhine, that would be dangerous for an enemy to pass. With these possessions, and with the consequent establishment of fortresses along the entire line, she would be almost impregnable on all sides, and could bid defiance to the combined powers of Europe.

This is the "Dream of French Empire," the attempts for the realization of which have so far proved abortive and unsuccessful.

STRATEGIC POINTS.

COBLENZ.

Coblenz is situated on the left bank of the Rhine and the right bank of the Moselle, at the confluence of those rivers. The name of the place is a corruption of Confluentes, by which the Romans called it. It is about seventy-five miles northeast of Metz by the post road, but is more than double that distance by way of the river, owing to its sinuosities. Coblenz contains a population of about twenty-five thousand souls, and is one of the best fortified places in Prussia. The fortifications surrounding it form a vast camp, capable of containing one hundred thousand men, and combine the systems of Carnot and Montalembert. Four forts protect it on the left bank of the Rhine. The first is Fort Kaiser Franz, situated below the town on the left bank of the Moselle, and commanding all the approaches from Cologne and Treves. Above, on the hill of the Chartreuse, are Forts Alexander and Constantine, the guns of which sweep the roads from Mayence. Fourth fort is situated over the Hundsruck Mountain. These fortifications, with the fortress of Ehrenbreitstein, after the downfall of Napoleon, were twenty odd years in rebuilding, and cost some $5,000,000. The principal strength of the city lies in Ehrenbreitstein (honor's broad stone), a village and fortress situated on a large rock which towers above every thing for miles around. It is termed the Gibraltar of the Rhine and is certainly a most formidable position. On three sides it is absolutely impregnable to assault, but on the northwest it is comparatively exposed. Its weakness here is apparent at a glance, and efforts have been made to repair it by the construction of three lines of defenses, all of which must be stormed before an enemy can enter the fortress. Nevertheless it is possible that artillery massed on these works could render them untenable. Four hundred heavy guns are mounted in the fortress, and these sweep the Rhine in all directions and the road to Nassau. On the top of the rock is a great platform which serves as a parade ground and which covers large arched cisterns, supplied with water by springs without the walls, and capable of containing a three years' supply of the liquid. There is also a well, sunk 400 feet in the rock, communicating with the Rhine. In 1794 Coblenz proper was taken by the French after a desperate resistance. Ehrenbreitstein, which the same nation had failed to capture in 1688, although Vauban himself directed the operations, held out until 1796, when it was compelled to surrender, the garrison having been reduced to starvation. Cats and horses were eaten by the besieged during the last days. It is hardly possible that any attempt will be made by the French to take Coblenz by a direct attack. A flank movement to drive the Prussians from the place will doubtless be made. After the peace of Luneville the French blew up Ehrenbreitstein on evacuating it; but it is now considered to be stronger than ever.

KREUZENACH.

Kreuzenach is a town of 10,000 inhabitants, and is situated eight miles south of Bingen ("dear Bingen on the Rhine"), on the railroad between Metz and Mayence. This railroad runs west by south from Mayence to Bingen, near the banks of the Rhine, when it takes an abrupt turn and continues almost due south to Kreuzenach, when it follows a west by south, southwest, and west-southwest course to Metz, making it a decidedly crooked road. It forms connection with the Metz and Mannheim Railroad at Bexbach, on the Bavarian frontier, where a single road continues to Metz. Near Bexbach is the town of Homburg, in Bavaria, where the fortress of Schlossberg, celebrated in the Thirty Years' War, was located, and which was razed in 1714.

Kreuzenach lies on both sides of the River Nahe, a stone bridge connecting the two parts. The west side, which is the most populous, is poor and dilapidated, but the east side is covered by splendid hotels and fine houses. On account of its cold saline spring it is a favorite resort for invalids, several thousands of whom visit it yearly. As a military position the place possesses no special importance. It is, however, very old, and was at one time a fortified post. In 1632 the Swedes, commanded by Gustavus Adolphus, took it by assault, after a severe struggle, in which Lord Craven, the champion of the Queen of Bohemia, and every English officer present were wounded. It has been owned alternately by the Germans and French, though it has been for the greater part of the time under the control or protection of France. In 1644, the French gave it to the Counts Palatine of Simmern, exactly forty-four years after they ravaged it; in 1807 it was annexed to the empire, and in 1814, after the downfall of Napoleon, it was given to Prussia, which country has retained it ever since.

The distances from Kreuzenach to the most prominent points occupied by the belligerent armies are as follows:—To Metz, about 116 miles by railroad; to Coblenz, about forty-three miles, via Bingen; to Mayence, via Bingen, about twenty-three; to Mannheim, by post road, forty miles, and to Treves about sixty miles. Its special advantage is undoubtedly its position between Coblenz and Mayence, and the complete manner in which it covers the entire railroad connecting those two places.

CARLSRUHE.

Carlsruhe is a city of the Grand Duchy of Baden, and of the circle of Middle Rhine, on the railway from Mannheim to Basel, four miles east of the Rhine, and thirty-nine miles west-northwest of Stuttgart.

Population, about 30,000.

MAYENCE (OR MENTZ).

Mayence is a city of Hesse-Darmstadt, capital of Rheinhessen, on the left bank of the Rhine, opposite to the mouth of the Main, and twenty miles west-southwest of Frankfort, with which it is connected by railway. It has a fortress, and is walled, and flanked with bastions, and defended besides by a citadel and several formidable forts and outworks. Fortifications have also been erected on some of the islands in the river. The famous bridge of boats 1,600 feet long connects it with Castel. Mayence owes its foundation to a Roman camp which Drusus pitched here. It was shortly after converted into a permanent bulwark, and became the most important of the line of forts along the Rhine.

Population about 42,000.

THIONVILLE.

Thionville is a fortified town in the northeast of France, in the department of Moselle, capital of an arrondissement, and seventeen miles north of Metz, on the left bank of the Moselle. Population about 10,000.

MERZIG.

Merzig is a town of Rhenish Prussia, twenty-two miles south of Treves, on the Saar.

ZIERCK.

Zierck is a walled town of France, in the department of Moselle, eleven miles northeast of Thionville, on the right bank of the Moselle. Population about 2,000.

SAARLOUIS.

Saarlouis is a town of Rhenish Prussia, on the frontier of France, thirty miles south-southeast of Treves, on the Saar. Population about 5,000. It forms an important border fortress.

BOULAY.

Boulay is a town of France in the department of Moselle, fifteen miles east-northeast of Metz, on the Kultzbach. Population about 3 000.

TREVES.

Treves, situated in Rhenish Prussia, is on the right bank of the Moselle, fifty-seven miles southwest of Coblenz. The river here is crossed by a bridge six hundred and eighty feet long. It is the oldest city of Germany. Modern Treves consists of the town proper, and is surrounded by walls. Population is about 20,000.

LAUTERBOURG.

Lauterbourg is a fortified town of France, in the department of Bas-Rhin, on the river Lauter, near its confluence with the Rhine, thirty-four miles northeast of Strasbourg.

SAARBRUCK.

Saarbruck is a town of Rhenish Prussia, forty miles southeast of Treves, on the Saar.

FORBACH.

Forbach is a town of France, in the department of Moselle, on the Nancy and Mannheim railroad, forty-three miles south-southwest of Metz. Population about 6,000.

METZ.

Metz is a fortified city of France, in the department of Moselle, at the confluence of the Moselle and Seille, and at the head of the branch railway from Paris to Strasbourg, one hundred and seventy miles east of Paris. Metz is one of the strongest and most important places in France. Population about 60,000.

ST. AVOLD.

St. Avold is a town of France, department of Moselle, on the Rossel, eighteen miles west of Sarreguemines. Population over 4,000.

LUXEMBURG.

Luxemburg, the capital of the Grand Duchy of the same name, is one hundred and fifteen miles west-southwest of Frankfort and one hundred and seventeen southeast of Brussels.

Its natural position is so strong, and the different powers into whose hands it has successively fallen have done so much to extend and improve its means of defense, that Carnot pronounced it the strongest place in Europe after Gibraltar. The town is divided into two quarters, the Grindel and the Pfaffenthal. The latter stands two hundred feet higher on a steep scarped rock, and surrounded by a strong wall, deep ditches, and a double row of formidable outworks. The most remarkable part of the fortifications, called *Le Boue*, consists of a rocky promontory, which commands the valley both above and below. Population about 7,000.

BINGEN.

Bingen is a town of Hesse-Darmstadt, on the left bank of the Rhine, at the influx of the Nahe, seventeen miles west of Mayence.

Near it the Rhine breaks through a mountain chain, and narrows to form the Bingerloch, a dangerous rapid at low water. Population about 5,000.

WORMS.

Worms is a city of Hesse-Darmstadt, province of Rheinhessen, twenty-six miles southeast of Mentz, on the left bank of the Rhine, here crossed by a flying bridge. Population about 12,000.

MANNHEIM.

Mannheim is a town of Baden, circle of the Lower Rhine, on the right bank of the Rhine, between it and the Neckar, in a low situation protected by a dike, and is sixty-six miles south-southwest of Frankfort.

NEUBURG.

Neuburg is a village of Rhenish-Bavaria, near the Rhine, fifteen miles from Landau. Population about 2,000.

LANDAU.

Landau is a strongly fortified town of Rhenish Bavaria on the Queich, eighteen miles west of Carlsruhe. Population about 13,000.

THE HOHENZOLLERNS.

FREDERICK WILLIAM, usually styled the great elector, and the founder of the Prussian monarchy, was born in 1620, and his accession to the electoral power in 1640, is usually regarded as the founding of the nation. He brought Sweden to terms, freed Prussia from her former subordination to Poland, kept Louis XIV. at bay, and even cut into his conquests, welcomed Protestant exiles to a free asylum, founded universities, identified himself with the liberties of Germany, and died in 1688, the year of the great revolution that gave constitutional liberty its triumph in England. His son, Frederick I., born in 1657, carried out his father's policy, furnished troops to the English liberators, and January 18, 1701, attained the darling object of his ambition, and with his wife, the sister of George I. of England, was crowned at Konigsberg. He died in 1713, the first king of Prussia. His son, Frederick William I. was born in 1688, and died in 1740, after a reign of twenty-seven years that so fully shows his shrewdness and folly, his honesty and his cruelty, parental carefulness and brutality. He left his son Frederick II., called the Great, over six millions of surplus money and an army of seventy-two thousand soldiers.

Frederick the Great was born in Berlin in 1712, and died at Potsdam in 1786. It is well to remember that he had English blood in his veins, and that his mother was daughter of George I. of England. His life is too famous to need notice here, and I pass on to his nephew, Frederick William II., who was grandson of Frederick William I. He was born in 1743, and died in 1797. He was austerely educated under his uncle's eye, but voluptuous and visionary, extravagant and arbitrary; yet his reign of eleven years was not without good influence upon the public spirit, the laws and industry of Prussia. His son, Frederick William III., was born in 1770, and died in 1840

Before speaking of his career, I will complete the record of the royal family and say that the son, Frederick William IV., who succeeded him in 1840, was born in 1795, and in 1858 he was compelled by insanity to yield the management of affairs to his brother William, who succeeded him in 1861, as King William I., who was born in 1797, and whose son, Prince Frederick William, born in 1831, is now the crown prince of Prussia.

FREDERICK WILLIAM III.

Frederick William III. deserves to be named with his grand uncle, Frederick the Great, as doing the work in the nineteenth century which Frederick did in the eighteenth. He withstood Napoleon and French centralization, with all its Latin affinities, as Frederick withstood very much the same spirit in the despots of Russia, Austria, and France, and fought the battle of modern times in his day. He was carefully educated by a good mother, saw enough of his father's extravagances and his grand-uncle's severe economy to form habits and ideas of order, discipline, and frugality. Probably the best thing for him was his early marriage at the age of twenty-three, to the beautiful and accomplished Princess Louisa, of Mecklenburg-Strelitz, whom he met at Frankfort in 1793. It seems to have been an honest, old-fashioned love match, wise as it turned out in the end to be, and the Prince of Prussia was so struck by her beauty, nobleness, grace, and sense, that he at once asked her hand. The betrothal took place, and the marriage followed on the 24th of December following. On the death of King Frederick William, she ascended the throne with her husband, November 16, 1798, and won all hearts by her goodness. She helped the unfortunate, interested herself in art and literature, encouraged agriculture and education, and had an eye for merit of all kinds. The favorite of the Prussian people, she had, of course, a certain influence in public affairs, and is supposed in 1804 to have influenced the king in favor of the war with France, which proved to be so disastrous to Prussia, although it was very popular with the people at the time.

LOUISA AND NAPOLEON I.

Austerlitz, Jena, and Friedland brought the humiliating peace of Tilsit, July, 1807, which sacrificed one half the territory of Prussia and left the other half at the mercy of the conqueror. Louisa was with Frederick William during that treaty, and there met Napoleon twice at dinner, and almost persuaded him, in spite of himself, to grant her request. The first time he presented her with a rose, and as she accepted it, she added, "*Avec Magdeburg au moins.*"—"With Magdeburg at least." She did not get that fortress from Napoleon, but he confessed that she was fully up to him in spirit, and led the conversation in spite of his efforts and his address, constantly pressing her point upon him with great propriety, and in a way that could not provoke him. The queen seems to have been a sharp thorn, however, to the French emperor, and there is reason to believe that he countenanced lampoons against her, and even accused her of too much regard for Alexander of Russia. One of his bulletins satirized the part she took at the tomb of Frederick the Great at Potsdam in the oath of her husband and Alexander against the French, November 4, 1805, and the consequence, which was the battle of Austerlitz and the evacuation of Germany by the Russian army with marching rations. Yet in the calm reflection of St. Helena he seems to have thought well of the brave woman who had done so much to set Germany against him, and whose spirit strove against him long after her exhausted body was laid to rest in 1810. O'Meara attributes these sentiments to Napoleon:

"I have had," said the emperor, "a high consideration for her; and if the king had brought her at first to Tilsit, he would have obtained better conditions. She was elegant, *spirituelle*, prodigiously insinuating. She bitterly deplored the war. The queen could not be consoled for the treaty of Tilsit and for the loss of Magdeburg. 'Peace is concluded,' she wrote a little time after, 'but at what price! Our frontiers do not reach beyond the Elbe. After all the king has shown himself greater than his adversary.'"

Napoleon had good cause to remember her as she was before and after her early death at thirty-four. She was with the king in his humiliation after his defeats, went with him to St. Petersburg in 1808 to share in the splendid reception there, and December 23, 1809, she re-entered Berlin with him, and took part in all his worthy efforts for the good of his people, and her name deserves to be connected with the foundation of that great Berlin University, which in some respects has no superior on earth. In June, 1810, she died in her husband's arms, and her body was laid in peace in the park at Charlottenburg, where Rauch raised a statue worthy of her memory, and where now her husband rests by her side in the tomb with a statue from the same masterhand. Her spirit never left him and the nation. She was with Blucher and the Prussians when they bore down upon the French at Waterloo, and settled the fortunes of the day; and even now the order of Louisa, which the king created August 3, 1814, after entering Paris in triumph, is the inspiration and reward of the young chivalry of Prussia, and led so many heroes in the sainted queen's name to the victory of Sadowa in 1866.

THE DESCENDANTS OF LOUISA.

It is interesting to remember that the eldest daughter of Louisa, the Princess Charlotte, was married July 13, 1817, to Nicholas of Russia, and that she was the mother of

Alexander II., the present emperor, a fact that strangely rebuffs the lampoon of Napoleon I. as to the oath of Alexander and Frederick William at the tomb of Frederick the Great in the queen's presence, and shows that Louisa's race still lives and triumphs, while Napoleon's seed has perished, in spite of his repudiation of his loyal Josephine and his shift to win posterity and fame by an alliance with the house of Austria. The Emperor of Russia is her grandson, the King of Prussia is her son, and the Prince Royal of Prussia is her grandson, with good prospect of perpetuating his race by his marriage with Victoria's daughter Victoria, who has already kept up the good name of her English mother by presenting her husband with five children in twelve years—three boys and two girls. The Prince Royal from his manly and somewhat severe simplicity, is a man very much after the Frederick William III. type, and who would wear a patch on his boot in case of a pinch in his country's fortunes. His race, the Hohenzollern family, have done wonders by their economy as well as heroism, and they need both virtues in the recent extension of their dominion, and the new and embarrassing demands upon their treasury.

GERMANY.

GERMANY presents three distinctive groups: The Alpine Region south of Danube, 45,000 square miles; the elevated terraced central portion, 100,000 square miles; and the level northern country, comprising about 100,000 square miles; making in the aggregate, 245,000 square miles, with a population of over 46,000,000 of inhabitants.

Owing to its important central position, Germany has almost invariably become the theater of all the great European wars, no matter for what cause begun. On the west, formerly its principal defensive positions against France, viz.: The Netherlands (Holland and Belgium), Alsace, and Switzerland, have been lost. On the central portion of the Rhine France cuts deeply, almost at right angles, into Germany, and the valleys of the Main and Kinzig rivers form an easy road for a French invading army. Hence such strong fortresses as Mayence, Coblenz, Luxemburg, Saarlouis, Landau, Germersheim, etc., cluster there as bulwarks against French invasion, opposed by a similar number on the French side.

On the southeast, Germany is protected by numberless projecting spurs of the Alpine system and the mountainous character of Bohemia.

The weakest point of Germany is the east and northeast frontier of Russia, where the Russian territory enters into the body of Germany like a wedge. Resistance to which the fortresses of Posen, Thorn, Konigsberg, etc., offer very little to invading force from Russia. Nevertheless the defensive military power of United Germany would be so strong as to deter all attempts at conquest and would be fully able to cope with combined Europe.

At the beginning of the year 1866, the Germanic Confederation consisted of 1 empire (Austria), 5 kingdoms (Prussia, Bavaria, Saxony, Hanover, and Wurtemberg), 1 electorate (Hesse-Cassel), 14 grand-duchies and duchies, 8 principalities, 1 landgravate (Hesse-Homburg), and 4 free cities (Frankfort, Bremen, Hamburg, and Lubeck). By the death of the childless Landgrave of Hesse-Homburg on March 24, 1866, it was annexed to Hesse-Darmstadt leaving only 33 states.

The Federal Diet on June 4, 1866, adopted the Austrian proposition for a mobilization of the Federal army. The Prussian representative declared he considered the Federal pact dissolved, submitted proposals for the constitution of a new " bund," and withdrew from the Assembly.

The two Mecklenburgs, Saxe-Weimar, Saxe-Altenburg, Saxe-Coburg-Gotha, Oldenburg, Anhalt, Schwarzburg, the two Lippes, Waldeck, and Reuss, Younger line, following, soon after Prussia, the confederation was virtually dissolved, after having lasted 49 years, 9 months, and 19 days, from its formation, or the first meeting of the Diet in November 5, 1816, to the 24th of August, 1866.

This, in connection with the serious complications engendered in the joint administrations of the Duchies of Schleswig and Holstein between Austria and Prussia, the former favoring the claim of Prince Augustenburg, and the formation of a defensive and offensive military alliance between Prussia and Italy, resulted in the war of 1866, which ended in the annexation of the Elbe duchies (Schleswig and Holstein) to the kingdom of Prussia, and the Austrian state of Venetia (Lombardy having been already added) to the kingdom of Italy; the establishment of the North German Confederation, and the formation of a union of the four South German states, with military and other alliances between the same.

The North German Confederation comprises, with Prussia, all of the German states north of the Main, and is the representative of the highest development of mental culture and the diversification of human labor of Germany; while the South German Union (of the states of Bavaria, Baden, Wurtemberg, and the remaining portion of Hesse-Darmstadt), with the independent states of Liechtenstein and Luxemburg, have been slower in the development of mental culture and exhibit less diversification of labor.

Practically, Germany appears only as a vast conglomerate of a multitude of petty states, and the present arrangement is not generally regarded in Europe as a permanent settlement, but only as a temporary compromise for avoiding new and serious complications. An eminent writer has said, " Germany is not a nation, but merely a geographical designation." Of the truth of the assertion, the reader can best judge.

The aspiration of the German mind was, is, and always will be—as long as the race exists and the language is spoken—for a German National Political Unity, embracing all the German States of Europe—embodying a freer liberty and a purer and nobler civilization.

EUROPEAN WARS OF THE CENTURY.

WITHIN eleven years the French Republic of 1789 had ceased to be. The tide of destiny had swept away the Directory, it had overwhelmed the Bourbons, the Girondists, and Robespierre. The triumvirate of consuls had only served to show that France possessed a man who was equally great as a general and as a statesman, and that she had no other fit to cope with his ability or his ambition. Thus it came that in the year of grace 1800 Napoleon Bonaparte was First Consul of France, and had just established himself in almost regal state in the ancient palace of the kings. The revolution had almost completed its circle, and was close upon monarchy again. But "France had not ceased to be revolutionary." "Conquest made me what I am," said General Bonaparte; "conquest alone can maintain me in that position." It was not sufficient that France should be prominent among the European powers, "it must be first of all, or it will perish."

TRIPLE ALLIANCE AGAINST FRANCE.

It was, nevertheless, the policy of Bonaparte at this period to affect a desire for peace. He made friendly overtures to England, and had the counsels of the Whigs prevailed they would have been accepted. But the great premier William

Pitt, convinced the Commons that it was impossible to confide in a republic which in ten years had committed more crimes than France had done during her entire existence, or in the word of a man who had never respected a promise, and who had alike violated engagements made with foreign sovereigns and oaths tendered to his own government. In reply to this, the three consuls issued a proclamation calling Frenchmen to arms in defense of the national honor. In it occurred the following: "The English ministry rejects our offers; the English ministry has betrayed the secret of its horrible policy to sever France—to destroy its marine and its harbors—to blot it out from the map of Europe—to degrade it to the rank of a secondary power—to keep all the nations of Europe separated by divisions—to monopolize the commerce of them all and enrich itself with their spoils." . . . . "It is no longer for the choice of tyrants that our nation is going to arm; it is for the guaranty of all they hold dear—it is for the honor of France." Russia, Austria, and England were banded against the republic, but neither the republic nor its chief were appalled. The British government alone had been voted a credit of thirty-nine and a half millions sterling, while the entire sum in the French treasury might have been counted by thousands. Bonaparte reckoned on the enthusiasm of his soldiers, and on the resources of his own genius, and, in this instance, did not calculate in vain. Leaving General Moreau, who was to some extent his personal rival, and who commanded troops whose attachment to the First Consul was but feeble, to deal with the Austrians on the Rhine, he resolved to attempt his great achievement of crossing the Alps by the route of Mount St. Bernard, and strike a blow at the allies in Italy. There has been in modern warfare no more striking instance of the power of a single will, and the contagious enthusiasm communicated by a great enterprise, than the passage of Bonaparte's army of 40,000 men from Switzerland to the plains of Lombardy. The First Consul had not arrived a moment too soon. One of his generals was sustaining a close blockade by sea and land in the city of Genoa, another was retreating to the French frontier, and the Republic itself was being invaded by the Austrians.

BATTLE OF MARENGO.

Napoleon's descent upon Piedmont was as unexpected as it was sudden, and completely upset the calculations of the Austrian generals. They were equally unprepared for his further movements, and while they hastened to defend Turin from an expected attack, he had promptly invested Milan, and with characteristic energy proceeded to reorganize the Cisalpine Republic. Advancing from Milan to the relief of Genoa, of whose surrender he had not been apprised, the First Consul crossed the Po at Montebello, and took up a position close to the open plain of Marengo. Learning then that Genoa had capitulated, his attention was turned to doing battle with the Austrians who were encamped at some distance in front of him. Fearing that they might escape him, he advanced from his strong position among the rocks of Stradella into the open country, and found to his great satisfaction that the Austrians had resolved upon battle. Melas, the octogenarian leader of the Imperial troops, began his advance, and Bonaparte prepared to meet him by forming his army into three distinct divisions, each stationed about three quarters of a mile to the rear of the other. The French had in the field, to commence with, 20,000 men, whose numbers were, some hours after the battle had commenced, re-enforced by a reserve of 10,000, under Dessaix, who had just arrived from Egypt. The Austrians advanced to the attack with 40,000 troops, confident of success from their superiority in strength, more especially in cavalry and artillery. The immediate prize of the victor would be the possession of Italy, and it was probable that the issue of the battle would change the destinies of Europe. Under such auspices the Austrian troops advanced early on the morning of June 14, 1800, upon the village of Marengo. The attack was made at seven o'clock; by nine the French columns were dislodged and retreating in disorder. Point after point was gained by the Austrians, and so certain did the result of the battle appear, that General Melas retired to refresh a frame that years had rendered incapable of supporting fatigue. The battle would certainly have proved a crushing defeat for Bonaparte had not the reserves under Dessaix arrived at a critical moment. That general judged from the appearance of the field that he could only assist in covering the retreat of his superior. "By no means," said Bonaparte, "the battle, I think, is gained," and rallying his scattered troops, as he well knew how, and by a dexterous movement changing his base of operations, he did gain the battle, and slept as was his custom upon the field of victory.

THE NEW COALITION.

The decisive conflict of Marengo paved the way for an interval of peace, of which France stood urgently in need. During an almost uninterrupted struggle for ten years, she had defied, single-handed, the united strength of Europe, and was left by the treaties concluded with the various powers between 1801 and 1802, undisputed mistress of southwestern Europe. The treaty of peace with Great Britain is known as that of Amiens, and the failure to fulfill that portion of it relating to the surrender of the island of Malta was the reason alleged on the part of France for a renewal of hostilities. Hanover was taken possession of by the French armies, and the North German dukedoms were laid under contribution, the King of Prussia declining to interfere for their protection; Holland, Italy, Spain, and Portugal were compelled to furnish their pecuniary quota to the French government, and a further aid of $15,000,000 was obtained by the sale of Louisiana to the United States. The First Consul had been confirmed in his dignity for ten years, then for life, and still later on the 3d of May, 1804, the "Government of the Republic" was confided to "Napoleon Bonaparte, hereditary Emperor." After an interval of desultory hostilities, and the great demonstration made early in 1805, by forming a vast camp at Boulogne for the invasion of England, the emperor found himself called upon to face the powerful league of Austria, Russia, and England which the latter power had succeeded in forming against him. On the first of October he passed the Rhine, and entered Bavaria with an army of 160,000 men. "You are but the vanguard of the great nation," said the emperor; "if it be necessary it will in a moment rise at my voice, to dissolve the new league which British gold and hatred hath woven."

BATTLE OF AUSTERLITZ.

Advancing at the head of the main body of his army, Napoleon took undisputed possession of Vienna. He afterward proceeded to join the army that was advancing into Moravia to meet the Russians, and after being joined by other two divisions the French found themselves confronted on the plain of Austerlitz, on the road between Vienna and Olmutz, by the main body of the allies. The Emperors of Russia and Austria were on the field, and their generals commanded a combined force of 75,000 men. The French were about equal in numbers, and superior both in confidence and discipline. At sunrise on the 2d December, 1805, the battle commenced, and continued with varying fortune till sunset. The stubbornly contested field ended with the orderly retreat of the allies, after leaving, however, the greater part of their artillery and baggage, and an immense number of slain behind them. Its results were thus summed up by the victorious emperor: "Forty stand of colors, the standards of the Imperial Russian Guard, a hundred and twenty pieces of cannon, twenty generals, and more than 30,000 prisoners are the result of this forever glorious day. Their infantry, so vaunted and so superior in numbers, has been unable to resist your onset, and henceforth you have no rivals to dread. Thus in two months the third coalition has been vanquished and dispersed." The peace of Presburg followed the victory of Austerlitz, and by it the humiliation of the Austrian Empire became complete. In Italy and Germany alike it suffered a diminution of territory, and the emperor returned to Paris to receive the title of the Great, and to appoint subject princes to the kingdoms he had newly created.

NAVAL BATTLE OF TRAFALGAR.

Not content with his victories on land, Napoleon determined to dispute with Great Britain the supremacy of the ocean. On the 19th of October, the combined fleets of France and Spain, numbering thirty-two ships of the line, seven frigates and eight corvettes, left Cadiz under the command of Admiral Villeneuve and proceeded westward. The English admiral, Lord Nelson, having under his command twenty-seven vessels of the line, came in sight of the enemy near Cape Trafalgar on the morning of the 21st of October. The French admiral arranged his ships in one line, forming a crescent, converging to leeward, and so awaited the attack of the double column of British vessels that advanced against him. For four hours a desperate conflict was waged, each ship in succession having selected her adversary and grappled with her at close quarters. Early in the afternoon the Spanish admiral showed the example of retreat, and just as Lord Nelson's life was ebbing away from a fatal wound, received during the action, intelligence was brought to him that fifteen sail of the line had struck their colors, and that the fight had resulted in a glorious victory for the British flag.

PRUSSIA ARRAYED AGAINST FRANCE.

The Treaty of Presburg left Napoleon master of Western Europe. As emperor he ruled a France which extended from the Rhine to the Pyrenees, as king of Italy he controlled a territory extending from the Alps to the Adriatic; one brother sat on the throne of Naples and another on that of Holland. Spain was his vassal, and he held the position of self-constituted "Mediator" of the Swiss republic. Bavaria and Wurtemberg owed subjection to him, and fourteen princes, in all, in the south and west of Germany, formed what was called the "Confederation of the Rhine," and recognized him as their protector. The German Empire had ceased to exist, and Francis II. contented himself with the title of Emperor of Austria. Prussia had hitherto maintained a cautious neutrality in the struggle which had convulsed Europe. She had quietly submitted to some violations of her territory, and Frederick William III. had even treated with Napoleon for the cession of the Electorate of Hanover, the inheritance of the dynasty that, in the person of George III., then sat on the throne of England. The French emperor had no intention of keeping to this engagement, and an early intimation of how they had been trifled with aroused the utmost resentment in the Prussian government. On the 1st of October, 1806, the Prussian embassador presented the following demands: First—That the French army, without delay, repass the Rhine. Second—The establishment of the Northern Germanic Confederation. Third—The separation of certain places from the Confederation of the Rhine. The French emperor replied by a rapid advance upon Upper Saxony, with a view of cutting off the Prussian army before Russia had time to render them any assistance.

THE BATTLE OF JENA.

The Duke of Brunswick was placed in chief command of the Prussian army, and the veteran Marshal Mullendorf, the last of the generals trained under the Great Frederick, was second in command. On the eve of the 13th of October the hostile armies found themselves face to face at Jena. The French troops, numbering about 90,000 men, took up position on the heights which had previously been considered impracticable for artillery. The Prussians and Saxons numbered about 126,000, and were unduly weakened by the excessive length of the line occupied by their front. Two hours after day-break the action commenced, and for some time was continued with much obstinacy on either side. The turning point of the battle was an impetuous attack made by General Murat with his cavalry and cuirassiers. This turned the fortune of the day, and a complete and disastrous defeat of the Prussians was the result. The French bulletin claimed that their own loss amounted only to about 5,000, while that of the Prussians was represented by 20,000 killed and wounded, 30,000 to 40,000 prisoners, 300 pieces of cannon, and immense stores of warlike *matériel*. The French triumph was complete. Fortress after fortress capitulated to the conquerors; the chief cities of Prussia were soon invested, and a division of Napoleon's army, on the 25th of October, entered Berlin. The King of Prussia retired to Konigsberg to collect the scattered remains of his army, and the French, with little opposition, were allowed to take possession of Silesia.

THE RUSSIAN CAMPAIGN.

France was now on the very frontier of Russia, and the Emperor Alexander saw the necessity of making one great effort to check the advance of the victorious soldiers of the empire, and to prevent them becoming masters of the entire continent of Europe. The campaign commenced on the 26th of September, 1806, with the indecisive battle of Pultusk, and was continued in February, 1808, by repeated captures by both sides of the town of Eylau. At this place the Russians made the first successful stand against the French arms which had been done for years, and claimed a victory, whose results, however, they greatly exaggerated. It was not till the 14th of June, the anniversary of the battle of Marengo, that the decisive and sanguinary conflict of Friedland closed a protracted struggle by a signal victory for Napoleon. The later operations of the campaign had cost the Russians 40,000 men, twenty-seven generals, and 1,848 officers killed and wounded. After an interview between the Emperors of France and Russia and the King of Prussia, the Treaty of Tilsit was concluded, which changed still further the territorial distribution of Europe. Its principal articles were that the Prussian dominions on the east of the Elbe should be annexed to the new kingdom of Westphalia, that Prussian Poland should become subject to Saxony, and that the city of Dantzic, with the surrounding territory, should be restored to independence. On the part of Russia, it was agreed to recognize the Confederation of the Rhine, and that hostilities against Turkey should be immediately suspended. Thus was Prussia compelled to resign one-half of her territory and subjects, and more than one half of her revenues, while Russia was deprived of the previous existing barrier against the ambition of Napoleon.

THE PENINSULAR CAMPAIGNS.

In November, 1807, the French armies began to enter Spain. The Prince of the Asturias was induced to conspire against his father, Charles IV., and enjoyed a few months of royal dignity under the title of Ferdinand VII. In May,

1808, both kings were compelled to sign their abdication, and to renounce all title to the throne, and Joseph Bonaparte, who had just resigned the Kingdom of Naples in favor of Joachim Murat, the husband of Caroline Bonaparte, received the vacant crown. At the end of 1807, the royal house of Braganza, which occupied the throne of Portugal, had been conveyed under British escort to Brazil, and the Peninsula was left to the occupation of the Imperial troops to the estimated number of 120,000 men. Spanish patriotism, however, was aroused at the spectacle of the compulsory retirement of the native princes, and the whole country was soon ablaze with insurrection. The Spaniards fought as they had not done for centuries, and the soldiers of the empire received more reverses in a few months than they had done for years before. Portugal followed the example of Spain, and aided by the fleet of Great Britain and by arms supplied from the same source, the patriots became able to drive the French from several positions of importance. About the end of July, 1808, Sir Arthur Wellesley, afterward Duke of Wellington, led 14,000 British troops into Portugal. Re-enforced by further arrivals from England, he sustained an attack by General Junot on his position at Vimeira, and gained a victory which caused the French evacuation of Portugal. The year 1809 witnessed in the Peninsula a series of desultory engagements between the Imperial generals and the British troops, and an ill-organized struggle on the part of native patriots to regain possession of their country. A vigorous contest for the possession of Portugal commenced in the early portion of 1810, during which the military genius of Lord Wellington became still more conspicuous. The two following years witnessed a continuance of the protracted struggle, during which the battle of Barossa, the siege of Badajos, and the battle of Salamanca, yielded new trophies to the British arms, and added fresh luster to the military renown of their leader.

THE EXPEDITION TO RUSSIA.

During the Peninsular campaign of 1809, the Austrians seized the opportunity to make an effort to regain their lost territories. The peace of Tilsit had left Prussia reduced by one-half, and the two feudatory kingdoms of Saxony and Westphalia were established as a counterpoise to the power of the house of Hohenzollern. Bavaria and Wurtemburg acted as a similar balance against Austria, while Russia, as yet comparatively untouched, was merely compelled to evacuate the Danubian principalities of Moldavia and Wallachia. The Austrian campaign of 1809 only resulted in a fresh occupation of Vienna by the French troops, and was ended by the sanguinary but indecisive battle of Wagram. The Emperor Francis was shorn of a few more provinces, and became more than ever subject to the dictation of Napoleon. Russia had to some extent profited by the territorial losses of her neighbors, and continued up to 1812, in her character of ally of the French emperor. Her opposition was first excited by the disastrous results which the commercial restrictions established by Napoleon against Great Britain began to have upon her trade and national resources. Resistance to the ruler of France seemed at this period to be more than ever hazardous. He held Prussia in a species of vassalage; the Confederation of the Rhine was his own creation; and he had repudiated the Empress Josephine to marry Maria Louisa, the daughter of the Emperor of Austria. In challenging hostilities with France, Russia had, therefore, to look to England only for support, with the questionable prospect of aid from the dissatisfied Bernadotte, whom Napoleon had himself placed on the throne of Sweden. Nevertheless, early in 1812, the preparations for a gigantic conflict commenced. One division after another of the French army was marched through Germany; the principal cities and fortresses of Prussia were garrisoned with French troops, and treaties of alliance were formed with Austria and Prussia. The Russian emperor, on the other hand, ordered a levy of two men in every five hundred throughout his dominions, and after coming to an understanding with Great Britain, awaited the onset of his formidable assailant. On the 6th of June, 1812, Napoleon crossed the Vistula, and, announcing his determination of restoring the Kingdom of Poland, invited the Poles to rally round his standard. The Poles caught at the bait, and assembled a national diet to proclaim the re-establishment of their ancient monarchy. As he advanced into Russia, Napoleon began to experience the effect of the tactics adopted by the enemy of burning and destroying every thing that lay in the path of the invaders. "Never," said Napoleon, " was a war prosecuted with such ferocity. These people treat their own country as if they were its enemies." Smolenkso, Viazma, and Borodino, became in turn the scene of sanguinary combats, followed by a doubtful victory for the French, and by a continuous advance through a country that had been reduced to a desert.

THE OCCUPATION OF MOSCOW.

Repeated battles proved as disastrous to the strength of the Russians as to that of their enemies, and it was resolved to abandon Moscow to the invader. Two hundred thousand persons, of both sexes, and of all ages and conditions, were withdrawn from the doomed city, and Napoleon, looking at the spires and towers of the Kremlin, was shortly able to say, "All this is yours." The French thus obtained possession of a well-provisioned city, affording safe and comfortable winter-quarters, and their emperor looked forward to the subjection of Russia by the opening of spring. But the retreating commander had left behind him men who were instructed how to act in this crisis of the fate of their country and of Europe. Now in one part of the city, and now in another, the terrible agency of flame was employed against the conqueror, and in spite of the combined efforts of the soldiers, and the shooting at one time of two hundred of the incendiaries, Moscow was soon converted into a rolling sea of fire. "It was the most grand, the most sublime, and the most terrific sight the world ever beheld," and the desolation of the city was still further increased by the exasperated conqueror giving his soldiers an eight days' license to pillage what remained. By the end of October the French army was in full retreat, with their supplies cut off and their progress harassed on every side by the various bodies of Russian troops who hovered around the roads leading southward. By the first of December the rigor of the winter commenced, and the soldiers of the empire had to face such hardships as have probably never been experienced in civilized warfare. Harassed by a sleepless enemy, deprived of regular supplies of food, and imperfectly clothed, the line of their retreat was marked by piles of dead bodies, and of the 300,000 to 400,000 men who had crossed the Russian frontier a few months before, not more than 50,000 repassed them.

REVERSES IN GERMANY.

The year 1813 was a fatal one for Napoleon. With the retreat from Russia his star began to pale, and the princes who had heretofore waited at his beck began to perceive that his day was over, and to desert the power to which many of them owed their existence. Prussia began the defection by uniting its arms with those of Russia and England, and Sweden shortly after followed suit. Yet the military genius of the emperor seemed at first as if it were to triumph over every obstacle. With an army chiefly composed of raw conscripts, he gained the battle of Lutzen, occupied Dresden and carried the war to the banks of the Elbe.

Austria endeavored by a conference at Prague, to effect peace at this juncture. The terms proposed by the allies, that France should be bounded by the Rhine, the Alps and the Meuse, were disdainfully rejected, and the quarrel was once more submitted to the arbitrament of the sword. Napoleon endeavored to drive the allies beyond the Elbe, and by the victory of Dresden seemed likely to succeed, but the successive defeats of his generals in Silesia, at Berlin, and at Kulm, deranged his plans, which were conclusively overthrown by the crushing defeat of Leipsic, in which the Prussians found their revenge for Jena. At Leipsic the Saxons and Wurtembergers passed over to the enemy on the field of battle, and the emperor was forced to retreat hastily toward the Rhine, only to find that the Bavarians, who had also revolted, wished to dispute the passage with him. On the 30th of October, 1813, his troops re-entered France, whose frontiers were menaced on the one side by the victorious British, who were crossing the Pyrenees from the Peninsula; on another by the allies, who were advancing by way of Switzerland, and on a third by the Prussians, under Blucher, who were advancing by Frankfort.

THE ALLIES IN PARIS.

Hemmed in upon every side, Napoleon stood boldly at bay, and seemed at one time likely to break the cordon of troops that surrounded him. One general was sent to intercept the Swedes, then marching through Belgium, another to stop the Austrians at Lyons. Italy was defended by Prince Eugene, and the fortresses of Germany and the Rhine were still commanded by French garrisons. The Prussians, under Blucher, were approaching the capital. They were encountered on the Marne and defeated; the Austrians, under Prince Schwartzenberg, were descending the Seine, when the emperor suddenly turned round and beat them also. But by and by the combination became too strong for him, and after a brave defense of the approaches to Paris by Joseph Bonaparte, on the 31st March, 1814, the French troops marched out, and the allies marched in; the white flag of the Bourbons was once more set up; the Senate declared that Napoleon had forfeited the throne, and the people and the army were absolved from their oath of fidelity to him. At Prague the emperor had been offered the possession of France, within the Alps and the Rhine. When the empire was invaded, the allies were disposed to concede the possession of the ancient monarchy only; and now, on the 11th of April, 1814, he was compelled to renounce for himself and his children the thrones of France and Italy, and to receive, in exchange for the dominion that had extended from Cadiz to the Baltic, the small island of Elba, situated in the Mediterranean, opposite the Grand Duchy of Tuscany, and forming a territory comprising a district sixty miles in circumference, and having a population of 14,000 inhabitants.

NAPOLEON'S RETURN FROM ELBA.

Louis XVIII. had reigned but twelve months over a territory from which Belgium, Savoy, Nice, and Geneva had been shorn away, in which national pride had been deeply wounded, and where public disaffection became every day more difficult to repress, when the news went like an electric shock over Europe, that Napoleon had escaped from Elba, and with characteristic impetuosity was advancing upon Paris. Lyons received him with open arms early in March, the whole of Burgundy followed suit, regiment after regiment went over to his standard, and when Marshal Ney replied to the summons of his old commander, and carried over to him the army he had brought out to capture him, there was no choice but flight left for the Bourbons. Early on the morning of the 20th of March, 1815, King Louis went out, and late in the evening of the same day Napoleon once more took possession of the Tuileries. The Congress of Vienna found their labors for the re-distribution of Europe prematurely interrupted, and, before dissolving, they drew up a declaration, in which they maintained that by appearing again in France, Napoleon Bonaparte had " deprived himself of the protection of the law, and has manifested to the universe that there can be neither peace nor truce with him." A treaty was immediately concluded between Great Britain, Austria, Prussia, and Russia, in which the contracting parties agreed to maintain and enforce the Treaty of Paris, which excluded Bonaparte from the throne, and to enforce the decree of outlawry issued against him. Each of the contracting parties, moreover, agreed to keep constantly in the field an army of 150,000 men until these stipulations were accomplished, and until, by common consent, they should decide upon laying down their arms.

PRELIMINARIES OF WATERLOO.

These resolutions convinced Napoleon that no other course was open to him except to stake every thing upon one great effort on the field of battle. The enthusiasm at Paris scarcely came up to his expectations, and the Senate seemed more disposed to bargain about a free constitution than to second his efforts to reorganize the army. On the 1st of June the Imperial eagles were once more distributed by Napoleon to his officers. On the 12th of June he left Paris on what he knew to be a struggle for existence, saying, as he threw himself into his carriage, " I go to measure myself with Wellington." The plan of battle adopted by Napoleon was to divide the forces of Wellington and Blucher, so that he could engage them separately. The former had his head-quarters at Brussels, and was in command of about 70,000 troops, of which barely one-half were English, the remainder being German, Belgian, and Hanoverian. Blucher was posted in the neighborhood of Liege, his men resting upon the rivers Sambre and Meuse. By the 15th June the entire French army was in motion, Napoleon himself advancing to the attack of the Prussian position, and Marshal Ney being detached with 45,000 men to drive the English from their position at Quatre Bras. In the battle of Ligny, fought on the 16th June, the Prussians lost 10,000 men, and were compelled to retire before the advance of the French troops. The British, with some difficulty, succeeded in maintaining their position at Quatre Bras, but on being apprised of the Prussian defeat at Ligny, Wellington ordered a retrograde movement toward Waterloo, in order to recover his communication with the Prussians, and to resume the united plan of operations which Blucher's retreat had interrupted.

THE BATTLE OF WATERLOO.

On the afternoon of the 17th of June, 1815, the British and allied troops came on the field, and took up the position from which they were to contest the most momentous of all the battles of modern European history. Later in the evening, and during the morning of the 18th, Napoleon brought up his army. The hostile forces were posted opposite to each other, on two lines of a chain of heights running nearly parallel with each other, and separated by a valley whose average breadth was half a mile. The number on each side did not exceed 75,000 men. The action commenced shortly before noon, on the 18th of June, by a cannonade on the part of the French, which was instantly followed by an attack, led by Jerome Bonaparte, on the old Flemish villa of Hougoumont, which was held as an advanced post by the troops of Nassau and a party of British. After a very severe contest, the post was left in possession of the defenders, and a combined attack was made upon the British center. This ended disastrously for the

French, but a body of British cavalry, having proceeded too far in pursuit of the retiring column, were driven back with severe loss. Then followed the renowned attack of the French cuirassiers upon the infantry squares and artillery of the British right, an attack which, for dauntless resolution and sustained and desperate courage, stands almost unequaled among the achievements of the armies of the First Empire. A succession of frantic charges, met by unswerving and deadly resistance, soon reduced the finest cavalry of Europe to a mere handful of men, and deprived Napoleon of the only means by which he could have partially repaired the disastrous termination of the day. By six o'clock in the evening 25,000 men lay dead or dying on the field, but still the desperate conflict proceeded. Blucher was meanwhile forcing his way from Wavre, at a distance of fourteen miles, in spite of the efforts of Marshal Grouchy, who had been detailed to intercept him. By half-past six the second division of the Prussian army had formed a communication with the left wing of the British, and it became apparent that a desperate effort must be made to turn the tide of battle before they should effectually decide the fortune of the day. The "Old Guard" had up to this moment taken no share in the battle. They remained during the day drawn up under Napoleon's own eye, near the French center. At seven o'clock they were placed under the command of the dauntless and unfortunate Ney and received orders to charge. For the last time the shout of *vive l'Empereur!* was heard from the soldiers of a hundred battles, and the Old Guard advanced before a continuous storm of shot and musketry, only to hopeless disorder and death. "All is lost for the present," said the emperor, and instantly riding off the field scarcely drew rein till he was close to the frontier of France. Blucher and his Prussians did the work of pursuit most thoroughly, driving the discomfited men from point to point with all that intensity of animosity which both general and soldiers felt toward their French opponents.

THE PEACE OF PARIS.

Perpetual banishment to the solitary and rock-bound island of St. Helena, in the South Atlantic, ended the career of the man before whose name Europe had trembled for nearly a quarter of a century, and Louis XVIII. resumed his place on the throne of France. The treaty of Paris, signed on the 20th November, confirmed France within its present boundaries. The fortresses of Landau, Saarlouis, Philipville, and Marienburg were ceded to the allies, besides seventeen of the principal towns and fortresses of French Flanders, which were to be occupied by foreign troops for five years at the expense of France. A celebrated treaty, known as the Holy Alliance, was in 1815 concluded between the sovereigns of Russia, Austria, and Prussia, by which, under certain very sacred and mysterious phrases, it was supposed that these Powers united themselves for the repression of any revolutionary tendencies in their respective dominions.

The desultory and protracted struggle relative to the succession to the Spanish throne, and consequent upon the will of Ferninand VII., excluding his brother Don Carlos from the crown in favor of the infant Isabella, can scarcely merit the title of a European war. Neither can the French Revolution of 1830, which placed the house of Orleans on the throne of France, nor that of 1848, which re-erected the Republic; or, still again, the series of events which, in 1851–2, prepared the way for the Second Empire.

THE EASTERN QUESTION.

On the 2d of January, 1826, the Emperor Nicholas I. ascended the throne of all the Russias. His accession was notified to foreign powers in these terms: "Called to the inheritance of the dominions of the Emperor Alexander, the Emperor Nicholas inherits also the principles which directed the policy of his august predecessor, and he professes the same fidelity to the engagements contracted by Russia, the same respect for all rights consecrated by existing treaties, the same attachment to the maxims which insure the general peace, and of the bonds that subsist between the powers." In July, 1827, England and France signed with Russia the Treaty of London, binding all three to insure a settlement of Greek affairs in Turkey. By the Treaty of Adrianople, made with Turkey in 1829, Russia obtained a considerable accession of territory on the Black Sea, and disregarded her pre-existing engagement with the Western Powers. Successive advances made by Russia in her protectorate of her Eastern neighbor, and particularly her endeavor to close up the Dardanelles to other nations, were viewed in Europe with increasing suspicion and alarm. Probably the true cause of the western jealousy of Russia was her immense and continuous acquisition of territory both in Europe and Asia, additions which, between 1722 and 1850, almost doubled the area of her empire, and raised her population from 14,000,000 at the former date to 65,000,000 at the latter. In 1853 the Emperor Nicholas, in pursuance of the traditionary policy of his house, showed a disposition to extend his protectorate over Turkey into actual occupation. Originating in a chronic dispute concerning the custody of the holy places at Jerusalem, a diplomatic quarrel between Russia and Turkey was fairly commenced in March, 1853. Matters were brought to a climax by the demand on the part of the Czar for the right to extend his "protectorate" over 11,000,000 of Christian subjects of Turkey. Supported by England and France, the Sultan refused to accede to this demand, and the war, for which Russia had been for months steadily preparing, was openly begun by the passage of her troops into the Danubian Principalities in July, 1853.

In August, a few more regiments followed, making the first division of the army of occupation reach the number of 80,000 men. On the 4th of October, the Sultan issued his declaration of war, and by the end of that month a Russian army under Prince Gortchakoff, and a Turkish army under Omar Pasha, faced each other on opposite banks of the Danube.

DANUBIAN CAMPAIGN.

After a series of conflicts, which, with the exception of Citale, scarcely rose above the character of skirmishes, the first important operation of the campaign opened with the siege of Silistria, the chief town possessed by Turkey on the banks of the Danube. On the 14th of April the Russians had thrown up batteries of great power on the north bank of the river, and commenced the bombardment. Fifty thousand Russian troops were massed on the south shore, in addition to the batteries on the north, and the defenders of the city did not number over 10,000. Weeks passed away, during which a most tremendous cannonade, varied by frequent attacks and sorties, was maintained against the stubbornly contested fortress. After more than a month, the Russian and Turkish commanders had an interview, in which the former stated, with a view to prevent a further effusion of blood, that he had positive orders that the place should be taken, and the latter replied that he had orders as positive that it must be defended, and that he would not surrender it even if he had but a thousand men and all Russia was at the gates, headed by the Czar in person. On the 23d June the Russians were compelled to retire, baffled, from their work, and the defense of Silistria became one of the most heroic episodes of a checkered conflict. By the treaty of the 14th June, 1854, the Emperor of Austria

undertook to occupy the Danubian Principalities against
Russia, and the interest of the war centered elsewhere.

BEFORE THE CRIMEA.

The bombardment of Sinope in November, 1853, which
Russia claimed as a great victory, and the allies designated
as a shameless massacre, roused the Western Powers from
the mediatory position they still endeavored to hold on the
Eastern question. On the 4th of January, 1854, the English and French fleets entered the Black Sea, a proceeding
which put a stop to further negotiations. War was formally declared by France and England in March, 1854—a
war undertaken on the one side to preserve the balance of
power in Europe by preventing Russia from absorbing Turkey, and prosecuted on the other with the ostensible object
of defending the orthodox faith against Mohammedan aggression. Austria and Prussia held aloof from the struggle, contenting themselves with entering into a treaty of alliance
whereby they were bound to a defense of each other and of
Germany generally, whether attacked by Russia or by England and France. The Mediterranean now became alive
with transports and vessels of war, Gallipoli, Pera, and Scutari became centers for the rapidly collecting troops, and
Varna was transformed into one huge camp. Years of unbroken peace had rendered the British War Department
the most incompetent in the world, and throughout the summer of 1854 the movements of the troops formed a continuous series of blunders and delays. While time was being
wasted in the construction of useless camps and in general
inactivity by the allies, the Turks suffered a series of
reverses in Asia, at Kars, Kurekdere, and elsewhere, which
tended greatly to inspirit the Russians and to depress their
opponents. The expedition of the combined fleet to the
Baltic in 1854 only served to reveal the impotence of the
war vessels then in use against the granite fortifications that

faced them at Cronstadt and elsewhere. The capture of Bomarsund formed the one slender victory of the Baltic fleet, whose fruitless cruise was productive of great discontent among the sanguine public, who had expected them to humble the pride of the Czar.

THE CRIMEAN CAMPAIGN.

At length, in the autumn of 1854, the allied armies were on their way to the Crimea, where it was hoped a vital blow might be struck at the supremacy of Russia in the Black Sea. Between the 14th and 18th September the allies, numbering over 60,000 men, landed within forty miles of the great fortress of Sebastopol, which they had come to reduce, and opened a campaign in which privation and pestilence cut down far the greater number of victims. On the 20th September the Russians were found posted on the heights above the little river of the Alma, and prepared to dispute the further advance of the allies. Behind the earthworks in this strong position it was estimated that Prince Menschikoff had 45,000 to 50,000 men. The Russian commander had claimed that he could hold such a position for three weeks against 100,000 men, but after a brief but decisive conflict he was compelled to evacuate the earthworks which he had considered almost impregnable. On the 25th of October the Russians to the number of 30,000 men made a further stand at Balaklava—a battle forever memorable from the gallant and fatal charge made by the English light cavalry brigade upon the Russian guns. It seems very questionable whether this dearly-bought victory at all advanced the main purpose of the allies, the taking of Sebastopol, while the two battles of Inkerman which followed it, and success in which were found no less costly, could only have occurred from an entire misapprehension of the topography of the great fortress now under siege. During the winter of 1854, Sebastopol became the center of a formidable line of intrenchments behind which cold and disease were more fatal than the guns of the enemy. The spring of 1855 came, and still the investment continued without gaining any very decisive advantage. The fleets continued the bombardment, and the land force made one gallant attempt after another to storm the outlying defenses, with but indifferent success. At length, however, early in September, nearly a year after their first arrival, the combined assault by the allies commenced, and after a series of gallant captures of the Redan, the Malakoff, and other forts, the welcome news became known to the 200,000 men of Britain, France, Turkey, and Sardinia, who were posted around Sebastopol, that the great citadel had at length fallen. On the day before the final capture, 20,000 men of besiegers and besieged had fallen; the year's siege had involved the construction of seventy miles of trenches, and during that time 1,500,000 shells and shot had been fired into the town from the mortars and cannon of the besiegers, and the entire loss of men during these operations was probably not short of a quarter of a million. Driven from the south side of Sebastopol, the Russian general resolved to hold the northern heights, and, calling for, and obtaining fresh levies of men, he maintained himself during the winter of 1855-56 opposite the allied troops, who faced him on the southern section of the fortress, which was divided by a deep arm of the sea from the town and ramparts on the north. In March, 1856, the diplomatists assembled at Paris, with a view to discuss the basis of an armistice, and with April came the cessation of hostilities and a treaty of peace. It required, however, nearly twelve months of negotiations at Vienna and at Paris to arrange the basis of a lasting peace; and, after all, the thirty-four articles of the treaty left things very much as they were before the opening of the war, with the exception, perhaps, that Russia's plans of aggrandizement were proved to have been premature.

AUSTRIA AND THE HOUSE OF SAVOY.

The policy of armed neutrality followed by Austria during the Russian war, was not forgotten by at least one of the Great Powers engaged in it, nor was the alliance of the little Kingdom of Sardinia in that struggle destined to be without result in the territorial future of Europe. On New Year's Day, 1859, the French emperor let fall a few significant expressions in his public reception of the embassadors of foreign powers, that convinced the world of the imminence of a struggle between France and Austria. It had been the traditional policy of the House of Savoy to extend the boundaries of Sardinia to the east and south, and to aim at the erection of a kingdom comprehending northern Italy, with a future view to the acquisition of the entire peninsula. The overthrow of Charles Albert in 1848 put a stop to his projects in this direction, but his son, Victor Emmanuel, inherited his policy and his determination, and only waited the occasion to carry it into effect. This disposition on the part of the King of Sardinia was a source of endless disturbance among the dissatisfied Italian subjects of Austria, and gave rise to frequent acts which the Emperor Francis Joseph chose to consider as demanding either diplomatic or armed interference. Great Britain proposed a conference with a view to averting hostilities, but, as a preliminary, Austria insisted that Sardinia should disarm. The demand was refused, and on the 28th of April, 1859, a declaration of war was issued by Austria and her troops ordered to enter Sardinia. On the 1st of May, France announced her intention of supporting her ally, and of "preventing a blow being struck which would establish at the foot of the Alps contrary to the wish of a friendly nation and to the wish of the sovereign, a state of things which would subject the whole of Italy to a foreign influence." "The passes of the Alps," said the document, "are not in our hands, and it is most important for us that the key should be kept at Turin, and at Turin only."

EUROPEAN ASPECT OF THE STRUGGLE.

When the conflict between France and Austria was seen to be inevitable, the most extreme complications were, on good authority, predicted as about to result from it. It was said that an offensive and defensive alliance had been formed between France and Russia, and that between them they aimed at nothing less than reconstructing the map of Europe. The terms of the compact were even defined to be a restoration of Savoy to France, and the resuming of her ancient boundary; Sardinia was to annex Lombardy, and Russia was to take the Waldo-Wallachian provinces. By and by the exaggerated nature of these rumors was discovered, but the opening of the campaign found Europe still possessed by the gravest apprehensions. Russia certainly did stipulate to place a heavy army upon the frontier of Germany, ready to interfere, should the States of the Confederation interfere in behalf of Austria. England and Prussia began to draw more closely together, and kept rapidly increasing their armaments, in order to be ready for the very grave emergency. Austria defended her position on the ground that "Lombardy was during many centuries a fief of the German empire, and that she had received Venice in exchange for her Belgian provinces." "The second French empire," said the Austrian minister, "is about to realize the long-cherished ideas, for the throned power in Paris has informed the astonished world that 'political wisdom' will replace those treaties which have so long formed the basis of European international law. The traditions of the first Napoleon have been resuscitated, and Europe is not ignorant of the importance of the struggle which is about to begin."

THE CAMPAIGN IN SARDINIA.

On the 10th of May, 1859, Napoleon III. left Paris; on the 12th he arrived in Genoa, and on the 15th he arrived at Alessandria, where certain divisions of the allied armies were in position. The first battle of the campaign was fought at Montebello, on the 20th of May, by the allied armies, numbering 6,300 men, under General Forey, against 25,000 Austrian troops under Count Stadion. The latter were driven from the position occupied by them in the village which gave the name to the battle; and, though for some time insisting that they had come off victorious, the honors of the day were unquestionably found to rest with the allies. On the 21st May the passage of the Resin was made by a division of the Franco-Sardinian army in the face of the fierce opposition of the Austrians. On the 31st of May the allies, under the command of Victor Emmanuel, attacked the Austrians, who had endeavored to retake the position occupied by them at Palaestro. The Austrians retired, with a loss of 1,250 men. On the next day the conflict was renewed, with a similar result. Meanwhile Garibaldi had commenced his series of brilliant successes in Lombardy. At the head of a body of raw, ill-disciplined volunteers the old apostle of Italian unity achieved victory after victory against the trained soldiers of the enemy—victories to which the enthusiasm and patriotism which the hero of Caprera managed to inspire into his troops contributed in no slight degree. The last week of May saw General Garibaldi drive the Austrians from North Lombardy, and gain, by the possession of Como, the command of the entire province.

THE VICTORIES OF JUNE.

On the 3d of June the Austrians began to evacuate Sardinia, and meanwhile the French force assembled at Alessandria had begun to act on the offensive. The emperor caused the Ticino to be crossed by a corps under General McMahon on the 4th of June. They were immediately attacked by the Austrians, whom they victoriously repulsed. On the 4th a general movement was made by the French troops to occupy the left bank of the Ticino. The Austrians, finding that the passage had been surprised, sent across the river three of the army corps, who burnt the bridges behind them. On the morning of the 4th they went before the emperor to the number of 125,000, and attempted to bar his march toward the village of Magenta. A desperate struggle ensued, which was shortly transferred to the village itself, and at half-past eight in the evening the French remained masters of the field, and claimed to have placed 20,000 of the enemy *hors du combat*, besides securing on the field of battle 12,000 muskets and 30,000 knapsacks. Thus was Piedmont cleared of the Austrians, and the gates of Milan opened to the allies. The people of that city immediately rose upon the Austrians. Victor Emmanuel was declared king, and Lombardy was annexed to Sardinia. On the 7th of June the emperor and king entered Milan. On the 9th the victory of Melegnano was gained by Gen. Baraguay D'Hilliers, and, after a series of successes in the north by Garibaldi, preparations began to be made for the decisive battle which was to decide the fate of Italy. On the 23d of June the Austrians repassed the Mincio in force, and occupied the positions of Pozzalenga, Solferino, and Cavriano. On the morning of the 24th of June Francis Joseph was in command of 250,000 troops, and awaited the attack of the allied armies, numbering, it is said, only 150,000. Shortly after sunrise the assault was begun upon the Austrian position in the hills behind the town of Castiglione. The French, after a desperate and stubbornly contested conflict, succeeded in driving them into the small villages on the plains below. Step by step the ground was fought for by the Austrians, and as the day advanced the struggle became concentrated around the village of Solferino. About five o'clock in the afternoon, when the cannonade was at its height, a storm of rain and thunder and lightning broke over the combatants but delayed not the unflagging course of the protracted fight, and it was not until nine in the evening, after a conflict of sixteen hours, that the battle was over, and one of the most brilliant victories of modern times was gained by the Franco-Sardinian army. Of killed and wounded a spectator of the conflict puts down the French loss at 20,000 men, while that of the Austrians could not have been less than twice that number.

THE PEACE OF VILLAFRANCA.

After a continuance of hostilities without any very decided engagement, Napoleon III. and Francis Joseph had an interview at Villafranca, and there arranged, to the great surprise of the powers who were anxiously watching the conflict, the preliminaries of peace. The basis of the treaty was the resignation of Lombardy to the French emperor, who agreed to make it over to Victor Emmanuel, and the retention of Venetia by Austria, although it was agreed that that province should form part of the contemplated Italian Confederation, which was to be placed under the honorary presidency of the Pope. Italy was not, therefore, yet "free from the Alps to the Adriatic," and the Italians were not a little disappointed at what they considered an inconclusive issue of the contest. The Venetians vigorously protested against being left to the tender mercies of Austria, and addressed to the great Sardinian premier, Cavour, a vigorous remonstrance to that effect. Italian unity was, however, destined, a few years later, to receive assistance from a somewhat unexpected source. Humbled in Italy, Austria was destined to a still deeper humiliation on her own proper territory of Bohemia.

THE SCHLESWIG-HOLSTEIN WAR.

The events of Germany in 1866 would be but imperfectly understood without a reference to the question of the Elbe Duchies, which for a time united two Powers, shortly after to be engaged in deadly strife, in an alliance of apparent cordiality. Amid all the endless complications of this unintelligible quarrel, this much is clearly defined, that the territory of Schleswig-Holstein had come by a sort of mutual agreement to form part of the Kingdom of Denmark; that nevertheless the advance of commerce began to draw it closer to Germany, from which it was divided by a purely imaginary frontier, and to which it was impelled by a powerful element of German-speaking population. Hence it came that the cause of Schleswig-Holstein was taken up as the cause of the fatherland, and the two leading powers of Germany yielded, or appeared to yield, in 1864 to the unanimous and enthusiastic desire of the people when they took up arms to right the alleged wrong suffered by the Germans in the Duchies at the hands of Denmark. The war, such as it was, formed a mere driving back of the Danes from the fortified position held by them, by sheer weight of men and metal. After completing the joint occupation by the peace of Vienna, of the 30th October, 1864, the jurists and cabinets of Germany were greatly exercised over the legal and constitutional rights of the question. When the proceeding of electing a German ruler was first mooted, Prussia treated it with coldness, while Austria favored the claims of the Prince of Augustenburg. The Prussian crown jurists had declared, in October, 1865, after a nine months' inquiry, that the joint sovereignty was vested in Austria and Prussia, and that if the Prince of Augustenburg ever had any claim to the allegiance of the Duchies, it had ceased with the peace of Vienna. In January, 1866, Count Bismarck announced to the Austrian cabinet that the encouragement given by them to the adherents of the royal pretender to the Duchies was regarded by Prussia as an aggressive act, which it had a right to guard against. The Austrian government replied by vindicating their right to take an independent stand on such a question, which Prussia chose to answer, just then, in an evasive manner.

PRELIMINARIES OF SADOWA.

Disturbed by the enigmatical policy of Prussia, Austria began to arm. On the 24th of March Prussia informed the minor German States that, impelled by the armaments of her neighbor, she must prepare for the defense of Silesia, and must also endeavor to obtain guaranties for the future, which it was vain to expect from her alliance with Austria. Military preparations having proceeded on both sides for some time, both powers were shortly plunged into a dispute as to who had begun to arm first, and at length, on the 18th April, Austria agreed to the Prussian demand to begin again to disarm, on the condition that the other power would follow, step by step. In the mean time, an offensive and defensive alliance had been concluded between Prussia and Italy; and when Austria insisted on the necessity of making preparations for the defense of Venetia, although disarming in Bohemia, Count Bismarck replied that the disarmament must be general. The haughty withdrawal of Prussia from the meeting of the Federal Diet, at Frankfort, and new negotiations early in May on the Schleswig-Holstein difficulty, did not improve the relative positions of the two German powers. Matters were brought to a climax when at the sitting of May 9th, of the Federal Diet, Austria announced that her representative in Holstein had been instructed to convoke the Estates, in order to hear the wishes of the population of the Duchies as to their ultimate disposal. The Prussian general in Schleswig was ordered to march his troops into Holstein as soon as the Austrian governor should convoke the Estates. This was done and the Austrians, not being strong enough to resist, retired from their joint occupancy. At the meeting of the Federal Diet of June 11th, Prussia was charged with having disturbed the Federal peace, and on the motion of Austria, it was resolved, June 14th, to mobilize the entire Federal force, with the exception of the Prussian contingent.

THE SEVEN DAYS' WAR.

Immediately after the Federal declaration, Hanover, Hesse-Cassel, and Saxony were occupied by the Prussian troops, resulting in but one insignificant collision with the army of Hanover. The rapid occupation of the Kingdom of Saxony followed, and the Prussians began an advance with about 160,000 men into the Austrian territory of Bohemia. To meet this force, the Austrian general, Benedek, had mustered 190,000 men, and the South German contingent of 150,000 men was daily expected. On the 30th June King William took command of his combined forces at Reichenberg. It was intended to give the troops a few days' rest, but on 2d July it became evident from the movements of General Benedek that an immediate attack was meditated by the Austrians. On the morning of the 13th July it was resolved to anticipate the Austrian general by being the first to assume the offensive, and Prince Frederick Charles advanced with the second army at 5 o'clock against the enemy. The first army commenced the attack at 8 o'clock, near the village of Sadowa, and at 10 o'clock the army of the Elbe advanced against the Austrians from Vechanstz. These were however, still much inferior to the number of the Austrians and it was not till the arrival of the vanguard of the army of the Crown Prince at 1 o'clock that victory began to appear certain. The superiority of the Prussian fire-arms had greatly contributed to bring about the result, devastating as they did, the solid columns of the enemy, and leaving the Prussians comparatively unscathed. By 4 o'clock, the Austrians were in full retreat, closely pursued by their foes. The total loss of the Austrians was estimated at 40,000 men; that of the Prussians at 10,000. Retreating to the left bank of the Elbe, the Austrians continued to fall back with a view to protect the capital. Another conflict ensued in the neighborhood of Olmutz, ending also disastrously for the Austrians, and as the Prussians advanced, there seemed every probability of their occupying Vienna without serious opposition.

THE PEACE OF NIKOLSBURG.

On the 17th of July, the quarters of the King of Prussia were established at Nikolsburg, and he was met by the French embassador, Benedetti, who was instructed by his government to make efforts to bring about a peace. The cabinet of Vienna was now convinced of its unreadiness to cope with Prussia; it had, moreover, a conflict with Italy to sustain, and the Hungarian Legion, under Klapka, was just then preparing for hostilities.

TREATY OF PRAGUE.

On the 21st July an armistice of five days was agreed on, before the termination of which the basis of the final treaty of Prague was mutually agreed upon. The most important stipulations in that agreement were that the Lombardo-Venetian kingdom should be united with Italy, that the hitherto existing Germanic Confederation should be dissolved, and a new organization of Germany formed without the participation of the Austrian Empire; that all rights to the Elbe Duchies should be transferred to the King of Prussia, and that Austria should pay forty millions of

Prussian dollars toward the cost incurred by Prussia for the war. Separate treaties were concluded with the South German States, each being assessed in proportionate sums to reimburse the Prussian treasury.

Such, briefly sketched, have been the chief national struggles and territorial changes of Europe during the present century. The series that began with the Napoleonic wars has not yet closed, but standing as we do upon the threshold of a struggle, whose magnitude may exceed any thing that Europe has yet witnessed, it would be premature to speculate upon the distribution of power at the close of a century which opened a vista of such endless and unexpected change.

BRITISH EMPIRE.

The British Empire comprehends two great divisions: 1st, The British Isles, or what is commonly called the United Kingdom of Great Britain and Ireland; 2d, Colonies and dependencies; containing an aggregate area of about 8,356,781 square miles, with a population of about 208,000,000.

The United Kingdom of Great Britain and Ireland comprises an area of 120,879 English square miles, with a population (1861) of 29,321,288.

The government is a constitutional monarchy, or limited hereditary monarchy, in which the executive power is lodged in the sovereign, but controlled in its exercise by the legislative power. The legislative power is vested in the Parliament, which consists of the House of Lords and the House of Commons. The House of Lords is composed of lords temporal (blood royal), British peers, representative peers not British, and of lords spiritual, and who (with the exception of four without seats) sit for life. The House of Commons is composed of six hundred and fifty-eight members, elected for one Parliament, which expires legally in seven years, but generally sooner. Its members are arranged as follows: England—40 counties, 144 members; 2 universities, 4 members; 186 cities and boroughs, 323 members; total, 471; Wales—12 counties, 15 members; 57 cities and boroughs, 14 members; total, 29; Scotland—33 counties, 30 members; 76 cities and boroughs, 23 members; total, 53; Ireland—32 counties, 64 members; 1 university, 2 members; 33 cities and boroughs, 39 members; total, 105;—grand total, 658.

The present ruler is Queen Victoria I., born in 1819, crowned in 1838. The heir apparent is Albert Edward, Prince of Wales, born Nov., 1841, and married March, 1863, to the Princess Alexandra, oldest daughter of the present King of Denmark.

Public Revenue, (in '67) £69,434,567 15s. 9d. = $336,063,308.

Public or National debt, £777,497,804 = $3,763,089,371.36,

ARMY.

The army in 1869 consisted of 139,163 men, divided as follows:—

Regiments of General Army.—Officers of General Staff, 7; Com. officers, 6,509; Non-Com. officers, 12,107; men, 110,885.

Depots of Indian regiments, including horse-artillery, royal artillery, and infantry: Com. officers, 392; Non-Com. officers, 974; men, 8,412;.

Recruiting and other establishments: Com. officers, 132; Non-Com. officers, 267; men, 76.

Training schools: Com. officers, 32; Non-Com. officers, 236; men, 10.

Besides these, the British army in India comprises 65,-

287 men, of whom there are: Com. officers, 3,615; Non-Com. officers, 5,306; men, 56,336.

The total volunteer force enrolled (in 1869), was 162,681: of which there are; light-horse, 662; artillery, 23,363; engineers, 2,904; mounted rifles,656; rifle volunteers, 134,096.

The number of enrolled militia to be called up for twenty-one days' training, is stated as 128,971 men.

NAVY.

There were in commission at the beginning of the year (1869), 152 vessels, all steamers, as follows:—Line-of-battle ships, 4; Iron-clads, 16; Frigates and Corvettes, 34; Sloops of war, etc., 98.

Of gunnery, training-ships, etc., there were 41 sailing vessels, and 57 steamers; also 10 steamers of coast-guard service, and 41 sailing vessels, and 18 steamers employed as tenders, making the whole number in commission as follows: sailing vessels, 88; steamers, 237.

There were afloat (in 1869), naval vessels of all sorts, 452 vessels, and 22 (all steamers, and all but 1, screw propellers) building, making in all afloat and building 474, of which only one-half were in commission; of these, 33 now afloat and 4 building were armor-plated (with ten-inch iron and seven-inch wood) and were of third rate; the remainder are of fourth or sixth rates, sloops, gun-boats, or floating batteries. 436 of the 474 were steamers, and no new sailing vessels were building, while those already built, 29 of 38 were mortar vessels and floats, and 7 were old-fashioned frigates, 1 a ship of the line, and 1 a sloop of war.

Of the armor-clad ships, 6 were of 6,000 tuns or more, 10 of 4,000 tuns or more, 4 of 3,700 tuns or more, and the remainder of various sizes, from 2,900 tuns down.

The three largest ships in the navy, are the Minotaur,

Agincourt, and Northumberland, driven by engines of 1,350 horse-power.

There are 37,015 seamen, 7,418 boys, and 16,400 marines employed in the fleet, making an aggregate of 60,833; and 2,950 seamen and 450 boys afloat, and 4,300 officers and men ashore of the coast guard, making a total of 77,700.

The English have now 35 iron-clad vessels either at sea or ready for it, and five more could be added to this number in less than three months—40 in all. Others, of course, are building or launched, such as the Sultan, Audacious, Invincible, Iron Duke, Vanguard, etc., and could soon be got ready. Still, in number, she would have five vessels less than the French, though in actual fact the fleet would be as one hundred to fifty, in consequence of greater size, speed, strength, and armament. The average speed of the whole English fleet is as nearly as possible twelve knots, the highest, the Agincourt, being fourteen and a half knots, and the lowest, the Vixen 8.894. Only four vessels in the list—the Enterprise, Vixen, Water-witch, and Viper, which are mere gun-boats, though armored and carrying heavy guns—are smaller than those in the French navy. Class for class, they immensely exceed the French in tonnage, thickness of armor, and number and weight of guns. The difference, on the whole, of the two lists may be represented between France and England as five to eight.

RUSSIA.

Russia comprises an area of 7,860,000 square miles, with a population of 77,008,446, and is probably the most extensive empire of ancient or modern times. It is bounded on the north by the Arctic Ocean; west by Sweden, the Baltic Sea, Prussia, Austria, and Moldavia; south by the

Black Sea, Asiatic Turkey, Persia, Independent Tartary, the Chinese Empire, and the Pacific; and east by the Pacific Ocean. Its possessions are—

1. Great Russia,
2. Little Russia,
3. South Russia,
4. West Russia,
5. Baltic Provinces,
6. Finland,
7. Kozan,
8. Astrakhan,
9. Poland.

The government is an absolute monarchy.

The administration consists of an Imperial Council, divided into five departments: legislative, military, civil, ecclesiastical, and financial; each department consists of 5 members.

The present emperor, or czar, is Alexander II., with title of Samoderzhets, or Autocrat, born April 29, 1818, and succeeded his father March 2, 1855. The heir apparent is the Grand Duke Alexander, married to the Princess Maria Dagmar, daughter of the King of Denmark.

Revenue (as per budget of 1869) is 482,000,000 rubles.

Public debt (1867) is 1,809,944,693 rubles.

Army consists of

```
        Officers........................................  30,507
776 Battalions Infantry............................ 538,877
583 Squadrons Cavalry.............................  63,440
200 Batteries of Artillery (2,000 guns)...........  80,172
        Engineers......................................  14,683
                                                        -------
                                                        727,679 men
```

Or nominally, on peace-footing, 800,000 men.

The army in time of war is divided into Regular and "Irregular" troops. The latter, in time of war, consist (in addition to the above) of 132 regiments and 24 battalions, with 200 guns.

The ratio of soldiers to population is,

In peace 1 to 500 males,
In war 3 to 500 males.

NAVY.*

Iron-clads.	Vessels.	Horse-power.	Tons.	Guns.
Frigates	11	5,510	43,287	124
Monitors	14	2,320	21,029	61
	25	7,830	64,316	185
Other vessels.				
Steamers	260	29,750 }	145,619	1,993
Sailing vessels	59			
	344	37,580	209,935	2,178

AUSTRIA.

THE Austrian Empire comprises an area of 249,048 square miles, with a population of about 35,000,000. It is divided into two portions, the chief frontier of which is the river Leitha : Cis-Leithan (western), and Trans-Leithan (eastern); the former is called Austria proper, and the latter Hungary—both being officially designated under one head—the Austro-Hungarian Empire.

CIS-LEITHAN PROVINCES (AUSTRIA PROPER).

1. Lower Austria,
2. Upper Austria,
3. Salzburg,
4. Styria,
5. Carinthia,
6. Carniola,
7. Goertz-Gradisca, Istria and Trieste,
8. Tyrol and Vorarlberg,
9. Bohemia,
10. Moravia,
11. Silesia,
12. Galicia,
13. Bukovina,
14. Dalmatia.

The aggregate population of the Cis-Leithan provinces, with army, etc., is about 20,000,000.

---

* In 1860 she had in the Baltic and Black seas—60 ships of the line from 70 to 120 guns; 37 frigates from 40 to 60 guns; 70 corvettes, brigs, etc.; 40 steamers; nominally carrying 4,000 guns; 42,000 seamen and 200,000 marines and artillerymen, besides a large number in the Caspian and Okhotsk seas and other waters. According to this statement there must have been a large reduction in number, with increase of first-class vessels.

AUSTRIA.

TRANS-LEITHAN PROVINCES (HUNGARY).

15. Hungary,
16. Croatia and Slavonia,
17. Transylvania,
The Military Frontier.

The aggregate population with army, etc., is about 15,000,000.

The government of Austria is a constitutional monarchy, the legislative department of which is vested in the emperor and two houses of parliament. The Upper House contains 11 princes of the imperial house, 56 hereditary members, who are chiefs of noble families, 9 archbishops, and 7 others having the rank of bishops, and 77 members appointed by the emperor for life.

The House of Representatives, consists of 203 members sent by the Provincial Diets.

In the budget for 1868, the receipts and expenditures were as follows:—

Expenditures........... 110,968,090 florins.
Receipts .... 10,610,900 "

Of the remaining deficit, 100,357,190 " the Cis-Leithan Provinces furnished 70 per cent., and the Trans-Leithan 30 per cent.

The provinces lost by Austria in Italy were Venetia and Lombardy, which now form a part of the Italian kingdom.

The present ruler is Emperor Francis Joseph, born August 30, 1830, and succeeded his uncle Ferdinand I. (as King of Hungary and Bohemia, called Ferdinand V.) on December 2, 1848.

THE AUSTRIAN ARMY.

According to official returns, Austria possessed at the commencement of last year, a standing army numbering 278,479 men on the peace-footing, and 883,700 on the war-footing, organized as follows:—

FRANCO-PRUSSIAN WAR.

Troops of Standing Army.	Peace.	War.
Infantry.		
80 regiments of line, each composed of 3 field battalions, 2 reserve battalions, and 1 depot battalion	121,840	485,440
12 military frontier regiments, 6 of 3, and 8 of 4 battalions	12,307	53,823
1 regiment or "Kaiser-jäger" of Tyrol, and 33 battalions of "Feld-jäger"	20,251	54,463
12 companies of ambulance and hospital service	1,180	3,876
Total of infantry	155,578	597,602
Cavalry.		
14 regiments of dragoons, 12 heavy and 2 light; 14 regiments of hussars, and 2 regiments of lancers	35,793	58,794
Total of cavalry	35,793	58,794
Artillery.		
12 regiments of field artillery, each of 14 batteries of 8 pieces	17,880	43,836
12 battalions of fortress and 2 battalions of mounted artillery	7,778	18,938
Total of artillery	25,658	62,774
Engineers and train.		
2 regiments of "Genie," each of 4 battalions	4,662	13,240
1 regiment of pioneers of 5 battalions	2,803	7,747
54 regiments of "Fuhrwesen" or train	2,401	24,147
Total of engineers and train	9,866	45,134
Miscellaneous establishments.		
Military instruction	2,234	2,234
Topographical survey	128	128
Commissariat and clothing department	3,705	7,200
Sanitary department	1,291	6,200
Arsenals, military stores, and buildings	3,000	4,500
Army studs	5,800	5,800
Military police and gendarmes	7,700	7,700
Total of miscellaneous establishments	23,858	32,762
Total, inclusive troops of reserve	278,470	838,700

The general staff of the army, on native service in 1869, comprised three Field-Marshals, eighteen Generals of Infantry (Feldzengmeister) and Generals of Cavalry; seventy-two Generals of Division, and 111 Generals of Brigade.

There were besides, non-active, twenty-eight Generals of Infantry and Generals of Cavalry, 150 Generals of Division, and 190 Generals of Brigade. The Austrian commanders are as follows:

1. Vienna, Baron del Monte.
2. Gratz, Marshal de John.
3. Prague, Prince de Montenuovo.
4. Lemberg, Marshal Neipperg.
5. Ofen, Marshal Jacobs de Kantstein.
6. Agram, Irinse Dietrichstein.
7. Brun, Baron de Ramming de Reidkirchen.
8. Innsbruck, ———— ————
9. Zara (Dalmatia), Marshal de Wagner.
10. Hermannstadt, Marshal de Rodich.
11. Veterwardein, Marshal Weber.

By the terms of the "compromise" come to between Austria and Hungary on which was based a new army organization, which came into operation last year, the military forces of the whole empire are divided into the standing army, the Landwehr or militia, and the Landsturm. The regiments of the standing army are under the control of the minister of war of the empire, and the Landwehr under the control of Austrian and Hungarian ministers. All orders relating to great concentrating movements of troops must emanate from the emperor, who is the supreme chief of the whole of the military forces of the empire.

The standing army is formed by conscription, to which every man is liable who has reached his 20th year. The term of service is ten years, three of which the soldier must spend in active service, after which he is enrolled for the remaining seven years in the army of reserve. Quite distinct from the standing army is the Landwehr, the term of service in which is twelve years, but with duties limited to the respective divisions of the empire from which it is drawn. The entry into the Landsturm, or general levy, is compulsory only in the Tyrol, and is made up of volunteers in the rest of the empire.

STRENGTH OF THE AUSTRIAN ARMY IN THE WAR WITH PRUSSIA, IN AUGUST, 1866.

Total strength, 646,098—viz.: 19,538 officers, and 627,098 men. Regular army engaged in active field service was 407,223 men—viz.: 10,932 officers, and 396,291 men. This strength was distributed as follows:—

	Officers	Men.
Infantry	6,686	249,243
Jägers	1,118	42,871
Border infantry	480	16,794
Heavy cavalry	312	7,008
Light cavalry	883	19,807
Artillery	513	22,245
And others	940	38,323

The casualties were:—

	Officers.			Men.		
	Killed.	Wounded.	Missing.	Killed.	Wounded.	Missing.
Infantry	428	1,138	352	7,997	21,545	32,710
Jägers	116	214	50	1,642	4,399	6,394
Border infantry	4	22	2	68	328	191
Heavy cavalry	10	33	23	148	205	890
Light cavalry	12	54	32	258	451	1,573
Artillery	17	44	20	292	868	1,231
Others	—	4	—	2	9	175
	587	1,505	483	10,407	27,805	43,264

STRENGTH OF THE NAVY.

The naval forces of Austria consisted in April, 1869, according to official returns, of 45 steamers and 10 sailing vessels. The following table gives the names of all the men-of-war, with their horse-power, guns, and tonnage:—

STEAMERS.

Iron-clads.	Horse-power.	Guns.	Tonnage.
Lissa	1,000	12	5,711
Kaiser	800	10	5,427
Iron-clad Frigates.			
Ferdinand Max	800	16	4,757
Hapsburg	800	16	4,757
Juan d'Austria	650	12	3,330

AUSTRIA.

	Horse-power.	Guns.	Tonnage
Kaiser Max	650	12	3,330
Prince Eugene	650	12	3,330
Drache	500	10	2,824
Salamander	500	10	2,824
Screw Frigates.			
Novarra	500	46	2.497
Swarzenberg	400	46	2,514
Adria	300	29	2,198
Donau	300	29	2,198
Screw Corvettes.			
Dandolo	230	22	1,594
Erzhezog Freidrich	230	22	1,474
Helgoland	400	6	1,635
First-Class Gun-boats.			
Seven, having each	230	4	852
Second-Class Gun-boats.			
Three, having each	90	3	333
Screw Sloops.			
Two, having each	90	2	501
One, having	45	2	348
Paddle Steamers.			
Sixteen, averaging	—	4	—

SAILING SHIPS.

	Guns.	Tonnage.
Frigates.		
Bellona	35	1,542
Vesud (Schoolship)	—	1,490
Corvettes.		
Carolina	18	860
Minerva	12	556
Brigs and Schooners.		
Montecuccoh	16	586
Arethusa	10	154
Arthemisia	8	167
Saida	6	269
Transports.		
Cameleon	—	143
Pylades	4	140

The navy of Austria was commanded in April, 1869, on the peace footing, by 2 vice-admirals, 4 rear-admirals, 14 captains of ships of the line, 13 captains of frigates, 14 captains of corvettes, 106 lieutenants, and 343 ensigns and cadets, and manned by 3,803 sailors. On the war footing, the sailors are to number 8,743 men and the marines 1,410. The navy is recruited like the army, by conscription from among the seafaring population of the empire.

Austria has twenty-four fortresses of the first and second rank, namely: Comorn, Carlsburg, Temesvar, Peterwardein, Eszek, Brod, Carlstad, Canove, Arrat, Munkacs, Cracow, Gradisca, Olmutz, Leopoldstadt, Prague, Brixen, Theresienstadt, Kufstein, Linz, Salzburg, Buda, Ragusa, Zara, and Pola. The last named is the chief naval fortress of the empire. In the naval engagement, during the German-Italian war of 1866, between the Austrian and Italian fleets, in which the former were victorious, the Austrian fleet was divided into three divisions, the first consisting of seven iron-clads, under command of Tegethoff; the second, of seven heavy wooden vessels, under Commodore Petz, and the third, of seven light wooden vessels.

SPAIN.

SPAIN comprises an area in Europe of 193,244 square miles, with a population of about 16,302,265; on the west is partly bounded by Portugal, and on the northeast by France; on all other sides it is surrounded by water, viz.: on the east, southeast, and south, by the Mediterranean and the Strait of Gibraltar, on the southwest and west by the Atlantic Ocean, and on the north by the Bay of Biscay.

Including its possessions in America, Africa, and Oceanica, it has dominion over 308,279 square miles, on which there are over 20,000,000 of inhabitants.

Possessions in Europe:

New Castile,	4	provinces.	Estremadura,	2	provinces.
La Mancha,	2	"	Andalusia,	8	"
Old Castile,	8	"	Murcia,	2	"
Leon,	3	"	Valencia,	3	"
Asturias,	1	"	Catalonia,	4	"
Galicia,	4	"	Aragon,	3	"
Navarre,	1	"	Basque Provinces,	3	"

Balearic and Canary Islands.

Possessions in America—Cuba, Porto Rico, and the Virgin Islands.

Possessions in Asia—Philippine Islands.

Possessions in Africa—The Presidios (Ceuta Peñon de Velez, Alhucemas, and Melilba, on the north coast of Morocco) and the Guinea Islands.

Possessions in Oceanica—Part of the Ladrone Islands.

At the head of each of the old provinces and nearly all of the colonies, is a captain-general (formerly viceroy). The old provinces are subdivided, making in the aggregate 49 new provinces (*departments*) each of which is under the administration of a *delegado del fomento*, and as to policy, under a *gefe politico*. The new provinces are subdivided into districts (*partidos*).

The communities (*pueblos*) are administered by elective municipalities (*ayuntamientos*) at the head of each of which is an *alcalde*.

The government of Spain has undergone a great many changes since 1812, and is a constitutional monarchy, being hereditary in the male and female line, until the late revolution, which ended in the deposition of Queen Isabella, and her abdication with the establishment of a Regency *ad interim* by the *Cortes* until an acceptable sovereign for the Spanish people is found. Formerly the sovereign was possessed of the executive power and of all the rights of sovereignty; and exercised the judicial power through judges, and shared the legislative with the *Cortes*.

The *Cortes* consists of two chambers, the Senate and Congress. The number of members for Congress is fixed at 271, each member must pay not less than $150 taxes; each one being chosen by 150 of the highest taxpayers in the district in which he resides. The senate consists of hereditary grandees, ecclesiastical dignitaries and life members appointed by the crown.

The Administration consists of seven departments and

Council of the State (Minister of the Regency, President, and 32 councilors).

The present Regent is Marshal Serrano, duke de la Torre, who was elected regent in 1868.

According to the *Annuaire de l'Economie Politique*, the revenue for 1869 was 258,200,479 *escudos*, or $12,406,992; and the public debt, 263,005,296 *reals*, or $12,262,425,29. Nearly four-fifths of the debt is interest-bearing, and latterly has undergone a small increase.

ARMY.

The Spanish army was reorganized on its present basis in 1844, and since which time up to the present date has been greatly increased in numbers and efficiency. It has a disproportionally large number of officers, who have exercised a prominent influence in the civil wars and contests of the country.

The army counts 10 captains-general (a dignity corresponding to the field-marshal of other European armies), 61 lieutenant-generals, 142 major-generals, and 375 brigadier-generals. The general staff consists of 3 brigadiers, 9 colonels, 12 lieutenant-colonels, 25 majors, 60 captains, and 40 lieutenants. The divisions of the army are as follows:—

ROYAL HALBERDIERS	283
INFANTRY.—40 regiments of the line (each having 2 battalions of 8 companies), 1 regiment *fijo* of *Ceuta* (3 battalions), 20 battalions of *chasseurs* (800 men each), and 80 battalions of provincial militia,	169,972
CAVALRY.—4 regiments *carbineers*, 4 of *cuirassiers*, 6 of *lancers*, 4 of *chasseurs*, 2 of *hussars* (each divided into 4 squadrons of 520 men each), 2 squadrons of *chasseurs*, and 4 squadrons	15,568
ARTILLERY.—5 regiments on foot, 4 brigades of flying artillery, 2 brigades of mountain artillery, 1 brigade of mounted artillery, and 5 brigades *fijos* on foot	12,369
ENGINEERS.—1 general inspector, 14 directors, 2 regiments of engineers (of 2 battalions each)	4,016
GENDARMES (*guardia civil*)	12,951
MILITIA.—Canary Islands (6 battal's of infantry, 17 comp's artillery)	7,329
CORPS OF CARBINEERS	11,784
CATALONIAN CORPS	516
	234,788

SPAIN. 133

Latterly there has been a large proportionate increase in the different branches of the service. The army operating in Cuba is included in the above. Besides the above there are schools of infantry, cavalry, artillery, engineer cadets, and for the general staff, and general military schools throughout the various departments or provinces. Spain possesses 125 fortified places, strongly garrisoned, twenty-five of which are of the first order in Europe.

NAVY.

Formerly the Spanish navy commanded all the seas, and Spain was the leading naval power of the world, but declined steadily in power and prestige, until recently, when a show of improvement was inaugurated. In 1861 the fleet consisted of 46 sailing vessels, viz.: 2 ships of the line, 84 guns; 3 frigates, each from 32 to 42 guns; 4 corvettes, 16 to 36 guns; 8 brigs, 12 to 18 guns; 1 brigantine, 6 guns; 28 vessels of smaller size; and 65 screw and 29 paddle-wheel steam vessels, among which is one screw steamship of the line with 100 guns. There were then in course of construction (but now completed and in commission) 2 ships of the line of 100 guns each; 2 frigates of 40 guns each; 8 frigates of 51 guns each; 8 schooners, and 8 gun-boats. Besides these, there were 111 ships for the defense of the coast, armed in proportion to their size, and 24 armed vessels on the coast of the Philippines. There were connected with the navy (in 1868) 1,121 officers of all grades, 189 paymasters, 93 mechanics, 12,976 seamen, 7,980 marines, and 539 guards of arsenals. Since 1868 a number of screw and paddle-wheel steamers have been added to the navy by construction and purchase, among which are some iron-clads of formidable proportions.

BELGIUM.

THE Kingdom of Belgium comprises an area of 11,373 square miles, with a population of 4,839,092.

The Provinces are :—

1. Antwerp,
2. Brabant (South),
3. Flanders (West),
4. Flanders (East),

5. Hainaut,
6. Liege,
7. Limburg,
8. Namur.

Each of the above provinces is divided into *arrondissements administratifs*, and *arrondissements judiciaires*; sub-divided again into *cantons de milice*, and *cantons de justice paix*.

Each *canton* is composed of several *communes* of which there are in the kingdom 2,514. Each province has its governor and council. The government of the kingdom is a very liberal constitutional monarchy, the legislative power being vested in a Senate and House of Representatives, the members of which are elected by the people.

The present ruler is King Leopold II., who succeeded his father, Leopold I. in 1865. The heir apparent is Count Philip, of Flanders, who married the Princess Maria, of Hohenzollern-Sigmaringin. Brussels, in South Brabant, is the capital.

Revenue, 169,403,280 francs.
Public debt, 717,155,214 francs.

ARMY.

The army in time of war consists of 100,000 men of the line, and civic or burgher's guard. Belgium has twenty-two strongly fortified places.

NAVY.

The navy is confined to a few steamers and a small flotilla of gun-boats.

Bounded on the north by Holland, northwest by the North Sea, west and south by France, and east by the Duchy of Luxemburg, the geographical position of Belgium places her, as it were, almost in the theater of the present war, making the preservation of her neutrality very trying and peculiar, not only to herself, but to the present contestants.

THE BELGIAN COMMANDERS.

Lieut.-Gen. Laurent Mathieu Brialmont.

This officer was born at Seraing, near Liege, in 1789, and is consequently eighty-one years of age. When seventeen years of age he entered the French army and served in all the campaigns in Germany, Spain, Russia, and his own country. On the restoration of the Bourbons he remained in the army and was employed by the government in the civil service for a time. Becoming disgusted with the Bourbons he resigned and returned to Belgium, which was then a part of Holland. Here he remained watching the progress of events and joining in the conspiracies for the independence of his country. He contributed greatly to the revolutionary movement of 1830, and for his services was appointed aid-de-camp to King Leopold I. soon after the accession of that monarch in 1831. General Brialmont commanded at Antwerp in 1837, and at Mons in 1840. He was appointed minister of war in 1850, and after leaving that post was made a lieutenant-general. In 1858, he was placed on the retired list, but was retained on duty as aid-de-camp to the king. The great age of General Brialmont makes it improbable for him to do much service.

Lieut.-Gen. Baron Pierre Emmanuel Felix Chazal.

General Chazal is a Frenchman by birth. He was born at Tarbes (Hautes Pyrenees) in 1808. After the restoration of the Bourbons, his father, who had been a member of the revolutionary convention which condemned the king to death, fled to Belgium, where he died in exile. His son received a good education at Brussels, and on the outbreak of the revolution against Holland in 1830 joined the revolutionary army. During the war he served with marked skill and courage, gaining promotion after promotion with surprising rapidity until he had won the highest rank. In 1844 the Belgian chambers accorded to him all the rights and privileges of a native " for eminent services rendered the state." After the downfall of the Catholic party in 1847, he entered the cabinet of Frier Rogier as minister of war. This position he subsequently resigned because of some reflections made in the discussions of the army budget in the Chambers. In 1856 General Chazal was sent to St. Petersburg to congratulate the Czar Alexander on his succession to the throne. At the present time he is an aid-de-camp to the king and a minister of state.

HOLLAND.

The Kingdom of Holland comprises an area of 13,890 square miles, with a population of 3,592,416.

The geographical position of Holland is an important one in Europe; bounded on the west and north by the North Sea; on the east, by Hanover and Prussia; on the south, by Belgium. The river Ems marks the boundary toward Hanover.

PROVINCES (IN EUROPE).

North Brabant, Gelderland, South Holland, North Holland, Zealand, Utrecht, Friesland, Overyssel, Groningen, Dreuthe, and Limburg; and with dependencies in Asia, Africa, and America, making an aggregate area of 627,558 square miles.

The chief cities are the Hague (or 'S Gravenhaag), Amsterdam, and Rotterdam.

The government is a constitutional monarchy, wholly vested in the king, who shares it with the States General, which consists of two chambers. The members of the Upper House consist of twenty-three named by the king for life; and of the Lower House of fifty-five elected by the Provincial States. The present ruler is King William III., born February 19, 1817, and succeeded his father in 1849.

Revenue, 94,865,321 guilders; public debt, 968,243,913 guilders.

ARMY.

The regular army, in time of peace, consists of 61,318 men (1,669 officers included), of which about 10,000 are artillery; and 27,168 men are in the East India Colonies.

NAVY.

The navy consists of 135 vessels, with 1,325 guns.

LUXEMBURG.

The Grand Duchy of Luxemburg comprises an area of 990 square miles, with a population of 199,958. It is bounded on the north and east by Rhenish Prussia; south, by France; and west by Belgium. Luxemburg, the capital, contains a strong fortress, and is considered the most formidable place in Europe after Gibraltar. It is 115 miles southwest of Frankfort, and 117 miles southeast from Brussels; a portion of the town is on a steep, scarped rock, 200 feet high, surrounded by a strong wall, deep ditch, and a double row of formidable outworks. Luxemburg is united with Holland by a "Personal Union," but has an independent constitution and administration. The government is appointed by the King of Holland. For administrative purposes it is divided into three districts, Luxemburg, Crevenmacher, and Diedrich, containing eleven cantons.

The present ruler is Prince Henry, brother of the King of Holland, governor since 1850.

Revenue, 4,836,220 francs; public debt, 12,000,000 francs, reduced annually 600,000 francs.

The army consists of thirteen officers, and 500 under-officers and privates, with one corps gendarmes, consisting of three officers, twenty-seven under-officers, and seventy-nine gendarmes; total 622 men.

ITALY.

The United Kingdom of Italy now comprises an area of 118,356 square miles, with a population of 24,273,776, and takes in the whole of Italy, except the Papal States and the Republic of San Marino.

In 1866 the following states were taken from Austria and the Pontifical States: Venetia from Austria (Lombardy being ceded in 1859); and Romagna, the Marches, Umbria, and Benevento, from the Pontifical States, and now form part of the Italian kingdom.

Its boundaries are, on the east, the Adriatic and Ionian seas; on the west, the Mediterranean; and on the north it is connected with the European continent by the great Alpine system of mountains, from which the Appenine range stretches along the entire peninsula.

ITALY.   139

It is politically divided into 8,562 *communes* and parishes.

The government is a limited monarchy, the legislative power being vested in two houses of parliament.

The present ruler is King Victor Emmanuel III., born March 14, 1820, succeeded his father as king of Sardinia in 1841, and assumed his title of King of Italy in 1861.

The revenue in 1869, was $142,373,411, and the public debt, $1,287,327,550.

MILITARY STRENGTH OF THE ITALIAN GOVERNMENT.

The Sardinian law of conscription forms the basis of the military organization of the kingdom of Italy. According to it a certain portion of all the young men of the age of 21, the number varying from 40,000 to 50,000, is levied annually for the standing army, while the rest are entered in the army in which they have to practice annually for 45 days, and are then sent on unlimited furloughs, but can be called permanently under arms at the outbreak of a war.

The standing army is divided into six *corps d'armée*, each corps consisting of three divisions, and each division of two brigades; four or six battalions of "bersaglieri," or riflemen, two regiments of cavalry, and from six to nine companies of artillery. The actual strength of the army at the commencement of last year was as follows, according to an official return:—

	No. of men (peace footing).	No. of men on furlough.	Total (war footing.)
Infantry of the line	118,850	184,272	303,122
Bersaglieri	14,727	21,448	36,175
Cavalry	16,165	9,604	25,769
Artillery	17,202	18,162	35,364
Corps of Engineers	3,104	563	3,667
Military Train	3,454	7,151	10,605
Carbinieri	19,628	....	19,628
Administrative Troops	4,463	3,752	8,215
Military Instruction	2,964	....	2,964
Total	200,557	244,952	445,509

The army was commanded, in 1869, by 14,797 officers, not included in the above returns. Of these, 870 formed the staff, while 5,967 were attached to the infantry of the line, 890 to the Bersaglieri, 689 to the cavalry, and 965 to the artillery. Every native of the kingdom is liable to the conscription, and to be enrolled either in the standing army or the reserve.

NAVAL FORCES OF ITALY.

The navy consisted, at the commencement of last year, of 99 ships of war, armed with 1,032 guns. They were classed as follows:—

	Number.	Guns.	Horse-power.
Iron-clads	22	272	11,380
Screw steamers	35	508	9,940
Paddle steamers	33	122	7,850
Sailing vessels	9	130	....
Total	99	1,032	29,170

The following table gives the names, the horse-power, number of guns, crew, and tonnage of the principal ships of the Italian fleet of war:—

Names of Ships.	Horse-power.	Guns.	Crews.	Tonnage.
Re di Portogallo	800	30	550	5,700
Ancona	700	26	484	4,250
Regina Maria Pia	700	26	484	4,250
Castelfidardo	700	26	484	4,250
St. Martina	700	26	484	4,250
Messaggiere	350	2	103	1,000
Frigates.				
Mary Adelaide	600	32	550	3,459
Duca di Genoa	600	50	550	3,515
Carlo Alberto	400	50	580	3,200
Vittorio Emanuele	500	49	580	3,680
Garibaldi	450	51	580	3,501
Principe Umberto	600	50	580	3,415
Gaeta	450	51	580	3,980
Corvettes.				
St. Giovanni	220	20	345	1,780
Governolo	450	12	260	1,700
Guiscardo	300	6	190	1,400
Ettore Fieramosca	300	6	190	1,400
Principe Carignano	700	22	440	4,086
Terrible	400	20	356	2,000
Formidabile	400	20	356	2,700
Varese	300	4	108	2,000
Esploratore	350	2	108	1,000
Sirena	120	3	63	354

The navy was manned in 1869 by 11,913 sailors and 660 engineers and workingmen, with 1,271 officers, of whom 2 were admirals, 5 vice-admirals, 12 rear-admirals, and 104 captains. The marines consisted of 2 regiments, comprising 234 officers and 5,688 soldiers.

SAN MARINO.

The Republic of San Marino, in Italy, forms one of the smallest and most ancient states in Europe, and is inclosed on all sides by the Papal States. It comprises an area of 22 square miles, with a population of about 8,000. San Marino, the capital, is accessible by only one road, and has three strong fortifications.

The legislature of the republic consists of a senate of 60 members, elected for life, and chosen from the ranks of nobles, citizens, and peasants. The executive consists of 12 members who are popularly elected. Two *capitani regina*, or presidents, chosen every six months, and justice is administered by a foreigner, appointed for three years. Two legal functionaries and two secretaries of state are the other public officers. The present *capitani regina* unknown. The public revenue is $6,600 annually: no public debt.

The army consists of 80 men, forming a guard for the regency, besides small garrisons in the forts.

PONTIFICAL STATES.

The Pontifical or Papal States include an area of 4,552 square miles, with a population of 723,121, and comprises the central part of the Italian Peninsula; bounded on the east by the Adriatic; southeast by Naples; southwest by the Mediterranean; west by Tuscany; and northwest by Modena.

The government is of a peculiar kind, partaking somewhat of the character of an elective monarchy, and is administered by Boards, or *Congregazionia*, with the Cardinal-Secretary of State, as prime minister, presiding. The present ruler is Giovanni Maria, Count Mastai Ferretti, born May 13, 1792; elected Pope, with title of Pius IX., June 16, 1846.

POLITICAL DIVISIONS OF THE TERRITORY.

1. Roma et Comarca.

LEGATIONS (*Legazioni*).

2. Bologna,
3. Ferrara (Ciacchi),
4. Forli,
5. Ravenna,
6. Urbino e Pesara,
7. Velletri.

DELEGATIONS (*Delegazioni*).

8. Ancona,
9. Macerata,
10. Camerino,
11. Fermo,
12. Ascoli,
13. Perugia,
14. Spoleto,
15. Rieto,
16. Viterbo,
17. Orvieto,
18. Fresinone,
19. Civita Vecchia.

In 1866 Romagna, the Marches, Umbria, and Benevento were annexed to Italy, for which consideration she is to pay 20,642,292 francs, and an annual *Rente* of 18,627,773 *lire* (*lira* 19 cents).

The Papal Revenue is (1868) 28,845,359 lire, and the Public Debt (1867) 37,402,695 *lire-rente*.

The army, in 1867, numbered nearly 10,000 men as follows:—

```
1 regiment of the line (Italians).......................... 1,850
1 battalion Cacciatori (Italians)..........................   800
1     "     Zouaves (French and Belgians)..................   750
1     "     carabinieri (Swiss)............................   650
1     "     troop St. Patrick (Irish) .....................   600
1     "     garrison troops................................   650
1 legion gendarmes........................................ 2,700
                                                           ------
       Total infantry.................................... 8,000
```

```
2 squadrons gendarmes............................  300
2    "    dragoons (partly foreigners)............  250
          Total cavalry.............................       550
1 regiment artillery..............................  800
1 corps engineers.................................  150
Staff.............................................   88
                                                        1,038
          Total.................................... 9,588
```

In 1869 there was a proportionate increase in the above, making an aggregate of 16,334 men.

PAPAL INFALLIBILITY.

DOGMATIC DECREE ON THE CHURCH OF CHRIST, PASSED JULY 18, 1870.

Pius, Bishop, Servant of the Servants of God, with the approbation of the Holy Council, for a perpetual remembrance hereof.

The eternal shepherd and bishop of our souls, in order to render perpetual the saving work of his redemption, resolved to build the holy church, in which, as in the house of the living God, all the faithful should be united by the bond of the same faith and charity. For which reason, before he was glorified, he prayed the Father, not for the apostles alone, but for all those who, through their word, would believe in him, that they all might be one as the Son himself and the Father are one (John xvii. 1–20). Wherefore, even as he sent the apostles, whom he had chosen from the world as he had been sent by the Father, so he willed that there should be pastors and teachers in his church even to the consummation of the world. Moreover, to the end that the episcopal body itself might be one and undivided, and that the entire multitude of believers might be preserved in oneness of faith and of communion, through priests cleaving mutually together, he placed the blessed Peter before the other apostles, and established in him a perpetual principle of this twofold unity, and a visible foundation on whose strength "the eternal temple might be built and in whose firm faith the church might rise upward until her summit reach the heavens" (St. Leo the Great, Sermon iv. [or iii.], chapter 2, on Christmas). Now, seeing that in order to overthrow, if possible, the church, the powers of hell on every side, and with a hatred which increases day by day, are assailing her foundation which was placed by God, we therefore, for the preservation, the safety, and the increase of the Catholic flock, and with the approbation of the sacred council, have judged it necessary to set forth the doctrine which, according to the ancient and constant faith of the universal church, all the faithful must believe and hold, touching the institution, the perpetuity, and the nature of the sacred apostolic primacy, in which stands the power and strength of the entire church; and to proscribe and condemn the contrary errors so hurtful to the flock of the Lord.

Of the Institution of the Apostolic Primacy in the Blessed Peter.

We teach, therefore, and declare that, according to the testimonies of the Gospel, the primacy of jurisdiction over the whole church of God was promised and given immediately and directly to blessed Peter, the apostle, by Christ our Lord. For it was to Simon alone, to whom he had already said, "Thou shalt be called Cephas" (John i. 42), that, after he had professed his faith, "Thou art Christ, the Son of the living God," our Lord said, "Blessed art thou, Simon Bar-Jona; because flesh and blood hath not revealed it to thee, but my Father who is in heaven; and I say to thee, that thou art Peter, and upon this rock I will build my church, and the gates of hell shall not prevail against it; and I will give to thee the keys of the kingdom of heaven; and whatsoever thou shalt bind upon earth, it shall be bound also in heaven; and whatsoever thou shalt loose upon earth, it shall be loosed also in heaven" (Matthew xvi. 16–19). And it was to Simon Peter alone that Jesus, after his resurrection, gave the jurisdiction of supreme shepherd and ruler over the whole of his fold, saying, "Feed my lambs;" "Feed my sheep" (John xxi. 15–17). To this doctrine so clearly set forth in the sacred Scriptures, as the Catholic Church has always understood it, are plainly opposed the perverse opinions of those who, distorting the form of government established in his church by Christ our Lord, deny that Peter alone above the other apostles, whether taken separately one by one or all together, was endowed by Christ with a true and real primacy of jurisdiction; or who assert that this primacy was not given immediately and directly to blessed Peter, but to the church, and through her to him, as to the agent of the church.

If, therefore, any one shall say, that blessed Peter the Apostle was not appointed by Christ our Lord, the prince of all the apostles, and the visible head of the whole church militant; or, that he received directly or immediately from our Lord Jesus Christ only the primacy of honor, and not that of true and real jurisdiction, let him be anathema.

Of the Perpetuity of the Primacy of Peter in the Roman Pontiffs.

What the prince of pastors and the great shepherd of the sheep, our Lord Jesus Christ, established in the person of the blessed apostle Peter for the perpetual welfare and lasting good of the church, the same through his power must needs last forever in that church, which is founded upon the rock, and will stand firm till the end of time. And, indeed, it is well known, as it has been in all ages, that the holy and most blessed Peter, prince and head of the apostles, pillar of the faith and foundation of the Catholic Church, who received from our Lord Jesus Christ, the Saviour and Redeemer of mankind, the keys of the Kingdom of Heaven, to this present time and at all times, lives and presides and pronounces judgment in the person of his successors, the bishops of the holy Roman see, which was founded by him, and consecrated by his blood. (Council of Eph. sess. iii., St. Peter Chrys. Ep. ad Eutych.) Peter in this chair holds, according to Christ's own institution, the primacy of Peter over the whole church. What, therefore, was once established by him who is the truth, still remains, and blessed Peter, retaining the strength of the rock, which has been given to him, has never left the helm of the church originally intrusted to him. (S. Leo, Serm. iii., ch. 3.)

For this reason it was always necessary for every other church—that is, the faithful of all countries—to have recourse to the Roman Church on account of its superior headship, in order that being joined, as members to their head, with this see, from which the rights of religious communication flow unto all, they might be knitted into the unity of one body. (St. Irenæus against Heresies, book iii., chap. 3; Epist. of Council of Aquileian, 381, to Grattian; chap. 4 of Pius VI., Brief super. soliditate.) If, therefore, any one shall say that it is not by the institution of Christ our Lord himself, or by divine right, that blessed Peter has perpetuated successors in the primacy over the whole church; or, that the Roman pontiff is not the successor of blessed Peter in this primacy, let him be anathema.

Of the Power and Nature of the Primacy of the Roman Pontiff.

Wherefore, resting upon the clear testimonies of holy writ, and following the full and explicit decrees of our predecessors, the Roman pontiffs, and of general councils, we renew the definition of the Ecumenical Council of Florence, according to which all the faithful of Christ must believe that the holy apostolic see and the Roman pontiff hold the primacy over the whole world, and that the Roman pontiff is the successor of blessed Peter, the prince of the apostles, and the true vicar of Christ, and is the head of the whole church, and the father and teacher of all Christians; and that to him, in the blessed Peter, was given by our Lord Jesus Christ full power of feeding, ruling, and governing the universal church; as is also set forth in the acts of the ecumenical councils, and in the sacred canons.

Wherefore, we teach and declare that the Roman Church, under divine providence, possesses a headship of ordinary power over all other churches, and that this power of jurisdiction of the Roman pontiff, which is truly episcopal, is immediate, toward which the pastors and faithful of whatever rite and dignity, whether singly or all together, are bound by the duty of hierarchical subordination and of true obedience, not only in things which appertain to faith and morals, but likewise in those things which concern the discipline and government of the church spread throughout the world, so that being united with the Roman pontiff, both in communion and in profession of the same faith, the church of Christ may be one fold under one chief shepherd. This is the doctrine of Catholic truth, from which no one can depart without loss of faith and salvation.

So far, nevertheless, is this power of the supreme pontiff from trenching on that ordinary power of episcopal jurisdiction by which the bishops, who have been instituted by the Holy Ghost, and have succeeded in the place of the apostles, like true shepherds, feed and rule the flocks assigned to them, each one his own; that, on the contrary, this their power is asserted, strengthened, and vindicated by the supreme and universal pastor, as St. Gregory the Great saith: "My honor is the honor of the universal church; my honor is the solid strength of my brethren; then am I truly honored when to each one of them the honor due is not denied." (St. Gregory Great, ad Euloguius, Epist. 30.)

Moreover, from that supreme authority of the Roman

pontiff to govern the universal church, there follows to him the right in the exercise of this his office, of freely communicating with the pastors and flocks of the whole church, that they may be taught and guided by him in the way of salvation.

Wherefore, we condemn and reprobate the opinions of those who say that this communication of the supreme head with the pastors and flocks can be lawfully hindered, or who make it subject to the secular power, maintaining that the things which are decreed by the apostolic see, or under its authority, for the government of the church, have no force or value unless they are confirmed by the approval of the secular power. And since, by the divine rights of apostolic primacy, the Roman pontiff presides over the universal churches, we also teach and declare that he is the supreme judge of the faithful (Pius VI., Brief super. soliditate), and that in all causes calling for ecclesiastical trial, recourse may be had to his judgment (second council of Lyons); but the decision of the apostolic see, above which there is no higher authority, can not be reconsidered by any one, nor is it lawful to any one to sit in judgment on his judgment. (Nicholas I., epist. ad Michaelem Imperatorem.)

Wherefore, they wander away from the right path of truth who assert that it is lawful to appeal from the judgments of the Roman pontiffs to an ecumenical council, as if to an authority superior to the Roman pontiff.

Therefore, if any one shall say that the Roman pontiff holds only the charge of inspection or direction, and not full and supreme power of jurisdiction over the entire church, not only in things which pertain to faith and morals, but also in those which pertain to the discipline and government of the church spread throughout the whole world; or, that he possesses only the chief part, and not the entire plenitude of this supreme power; or, that this his power is not ordinary and immediate, both as regards all and each of the churches, and all and each of the pastors and faithful, let him be anathema.

Of the Infallible Authority of the Roman Pontiff in Teaching.

This holy see has ever held—the unbroken custom of the church has proved—and the Ecumenical Councils, those especially in which the East joined with the West, in union of faith and of charity, have declared that in this apostolic primacy, which the Roman pontiff holds over the universal church, as successor of Peter, the prince of the apostles, there is also contained the supreme power of authoritative teaching. Thus the fathers of the fourth council of Constantinople, following in the footsteps of their predecessors, put forth this solemn profession:—

"The first law of salvation is to keep the rule of true faith. And whereas the words of our Lord Jesus Christ can not be passed by, who said: 'Thou art Peter, and upon this rock I will build my church' (Matt. xvi. 18), these words, which he spoke are proved true by facts; for in the apostolic see, the Catholic religion has ever been preserved unspotted, and the holy doctrine has been announced. Therefore, wishing never to be separated from the faith and teaching of this see, we hope to be worthy to abide in that one communion which the apostolic see preaches, in which is the full and true firmness of the Christian religion." (Formula of St. Hormisdas, Pope, as proposed by Hadrian II. to the fathers of the eighth general council [Constantinople IV.] and subscribed by them.)

So, too, the Greeks, with the approval of the second council of Lyons, professed that the holy Roman church holds over the universal Catholic Church a supreme and full primacy and headship, which she truthfully and humbly acknowledges that she received from the Lord himself in blessed Peter, the prince or head of the apostles, of whom the Roman pontiff is the successor; and as she, beyond the others, is bound to defend the truth of the faith, so if any questions arise concerning faith, they should be decided by her judgment. And finally, the council of Florence defined that the Roman pontiff is the true vicar of Christ, and the head to the whole church, and the father and teacher of all Christians, and that to him, in the blessed Peter, was given by our Lord Jesus Christ, full power of feeding, and ruling, and governing the universal church. (John xxi. 15–17.)

In order to fulfill this pastoral charge, our predecessors have ever labored unweariedly to spread the saving doctrine of Christ among all the nations of the earth, and with equal care have watched to preserve it pure and unchanged where it had been received. Wherefore the bishops of the whole world, sometimes singly, sometimes assembled in synods, following the long-established custom of the churches (S. Cyril, Alex. ad S. Cœlest., Pap.) and the form of ancient rule (St. Innocent I., to councils of Carthage and Milevi) referred to this apostolic see those dangers especially which arose in matters of faith, in order that injuries to faith might best be healed there, where the faith could never fail. (St. Bernard, ep. 120.) And the Roman pontiffs, weighing the condition of times and circumstances, sometimes calling together general councils, or asking the judgment of the church scattered through the world, sometimes consulting particular synods, sometimes using such other aids as Divine Providence supplied, defined that those doctrines should be held, which, by the aid of God, they knew to be conformable to the Holy Scriptures and the apostolic traditions. For the Holy Ghost is not promised to the successors of Peter, that they may make known a new doctrine revealed by him, but that through his assistance they may sacredly guard, and faithfully set forth the revelation delivered by the apostle, that is, the deposit of faith. And this their apostolic teaching all the venerable fathers have embraced, and the holy orthodox doctors have revered and followed, knowing most certainly that this see of St. Peter ever remains free from all error, according to the divine promise of our Lord and Saviour made to the prince of the apostles : "I have prayed for thee that thy faith fail not, and thou, being once converted, confirm thy brethren." (Conf. St. Agatho., ep. ad Imp. : a conc. œcum. vi. approbat.)

Therefore, this gift, of truth, and of faith which fails not, was divinely bestowed on Peter and his successors in this chair, that they should exercise their high office for the salvation of all, that through them the universal flock of Christ should be turned away from the poisonous food of error, and should be nourished with the food of heavenly doctrine, and that the occasion of schism being removed, the entire church should be preserved one, and, planted on her foundation, should stand firm against the gates of hell.

Nevertheless, since in this present age, when the saving efficacy of the apostolic office is exceedingly needed, there are not a few who carp at its authority; we judge it altogether necessary to solemnly declare the prerogative which the only begotten Son of God has deigned to unite to the supreme pastoral office.

Wherefore, faithfully adhering to the tradition handed down from the commencement of the Christian faith, for the glory of God our Saviour, the exaltation of the Catholic religion, and the salvation of Christian peoples, with the approbation of the sacred council, we teach and define it to be a doctrine divinely revealed ; that the Roman pontiff, when he speaks *ex cathedra*, that is, when in exercise of his office of pastor and teacher of all Christian peoples, and in virtue of his supreme apostolical authority, he defines that a doctrine of faith or morals is to be held by the universal church, possesses, through the divine assistance promised to him in the blessed Peter, that infallibility with which the divine Redeemer willed his church to be endowed, in defining a doctrine of faith or morals; and therefore, that such definitions of the Roman pontiff, are irreformable of themselves, and not by force of the consent of the church thereto.

And if any one shall presume, which God forbid, to contradict this our definition, let him be anathema.

PORTUGAL.

The Kingdom of Portugal comprises an area of 35,400 square miles, with a population of 4,399,966, and forms the western part of the Spanish peninsula.

Provinces in Europe.—Alemtejo, 3 districts; Algarve, 1 district; Beira-Alta, 2 districts; Douro, 3 districts; Estremadura, 3 districts; Minho, 2 districts; Tras-os-Montos, 2 districts.

Colonies.—Madeira, Porto Santo and part of the Azores; Cape Verde Islands, Guinea, Bissao, St. Thomas, Principe, Angola, Benguela, and Mozambique, in Africa; Goa, Bardez, Salsette, Damao, and Diu, in Asia; and Macao, Timor, Solor, and Midora, in Oceanica and China.

The government is an hereditary constitutional monarchy, under a constitution adopted in 1826. The legislative power is vested jointly in the sovereign and Cortes, which consists of two chambers, one of peers and the other of deputies. The peers are elected by the crown for life, and the deputies by electors.

The present sovereign is King Luis I., born October 31, 1838, and succeeded his brother, King Pedro V., in 1861.

The revenue, according to the budget of 1869, is 16,910,137 *milreis*, and the public debt, 220,868,202 *milreis*.

ARMY.

By an act of April 15, 1854, the standing army of Portugal was 24,000, with a reserve of 13,767 men. In 1869, the army consisted, in the kingdom, of 1,567 officers and 23,092 men; in the colonies, of 9,453 men of first line, and 21,411 of second line.

NAVY.

The navy now consists of about 26 armed, and 19 non-armed vessels, carrying 355 guns.

LIECHTENSTEIN (PRINCIPALITY).

LIECHTENSTEIN formerly belonged to the Germanic Confederacy, but since the establishment of the North German Confederation, in 1866, it has no relation with it, or the South German States.

It comprises an area of 54 square miles, with a population of 7,994.

The present ruler is Prince Johann II., born October 5, 1849, and succeeded his father, November 2, 1858.

Revenue, 55,000 florins.

No public debt.

Liechtenstein is the smallest principality in Germany, and is bounded on the northeast and east by the Austrian circle of Vorarlsberg and the Tyrol, south by the Swiss Canton of Grisons, and on the west by the Rhine, which separates it from the Canton of St. Gall.

The family of Liechtenstein is a branch from that of Este. The present prince has extensive domains in Moravia and other portions of Germany.

SWITZERLAND.

THE Republic of Switzerland includes an area of 15,722 square miles, with a population of 2,510,494.

THE CANTONS ARE

Aargau, Appenzell-Rhodes (outer and inner), Basel (city and county), Bern, Freyburg, Geneva, Glarus, Grisons, Lucerne, Neufchatel, St. Gall, Schaffhausen, Schwytz, Soleure, Ticino, Thurgau, Unterwalden (upper and lower), Uri, Valais, Vaud, Zug, and Zurich.

It is bounded on the north by Baden, from which it is for the most part separated by the Rhine; northeast by Wurtemberg and Bavaria, from which it is separated by the Lake of Constance; east by the principality of Liechtenstein and the Tyrol, from the former of which it is separated by the Rhine, and from the latter partly by the Rhine, but chiefly by ranges of the Grison Alps; south, by Italy, from which it is separated by the Alps, and from Savoy by the Alps and the lake of Geneva; and west and northwest, by France, from which it is separated by the Jura Mountains and the river Doubs.

The government is vested in a Federal Council (executive, seven members), Dr. Dubs, President, and Emel Walté Vice-President; a Council of State (forty-four members, two for each canton), A. O. Aeppli, President; and a National Council (128 members, elected for three years), Simon Kaiser, President. The President of the Republic is elected each year.

The revenue for 1867, was 19,781,961 francs.

THE ARMY.

The regular army consists of 87,730 men; the reserve of 49,765 men, and the Landwehr of 65,359 men; making a grand total of 202,854 men.

A military alliance with France, in 1868, was rejected.

DENMARK.

The Kingdom of Denmark comprises an area of 14,698 English square miles, with a population estimated at 1,717,802.

The dependencies are Faroe, Iceland, Danish settlements in Greenland, the islands of St. John, St. Thomas, and St. Croix in the West Indies, comprising in the aggregate, an area of 40,214 square miles, with a population of 108,983. The Elbe Duchies (Schleswig and Holstein) formerly belonged to the kingdom—and now form a part of the kingdom of Prussia.

The government is a constitutional monarchy, the legislative power of which is vested in the King and Diet jointly. The Diet consists of the Landsthing (upper house) and the Folkething (lower house), the members of which are elected by the people. The present ruler is King Christian IX., born April 8, 1808, and succeeded King Frederick VII., November 15, 1863.

The heir-apparent to the crown is Prince Frederick, born June 3, 1843, and betrothed to the Princess Louisa of Sweden, July 15, 1868.

The revenue in 1867 was 438,748 rix-dollars, and the public debt, 132,685,400 rix-dollars.

The army of Denmark in 1868, was composed as follows:

| | FIRST CALL. | | SECOND CALL. | |
	Officers.	Men.	Officers.	Men.
Infantry	730	26,750	235	9,396
Cavalry	126	1,922	...	...
Artillery	139	6,523	23	1,540
Engineers	...	...	4	207
	995	35,195	262	11,143

(LINE AND RESERVE)

The fleet, in 1867, consisted of 30 steamers (inclusive of 6 iron-clads, with an aggregate of 389 guns), 1 sailing vessel, 22 gun-boats, and 31 transports.

NORWAY AND SWEDEN.

NORWAY.

THE area of Norway is estimated at 123,386 square miles, with a population of 1,701,478; and the boundaries are, on the northeast, Russian Lapland, on the east Sweden, on the north the Arctic Ocean, on the northwest and west the Atlantic Ocean and the North Sea, and on the south the Skager-Rack.

Provinces—Aggershuus, or Christiania, Christiansand, Bergen, Trondhjem, and Tromsoe.

The government is a limited hereditary monarchy united with Sweden as a free, independent, indivisible kingdom.

The *Storthing* (legislative assembly) is elected by the people, and exists for three years, when a new election takes place. It is composed of two chambers—the *Lagthing*, numbering one-fourth of the members, and the *Odelsthing* three-fourths.

According to the Norwegian budget of 1869, the revenue consisted of 5,023,000 specie dollars, and the public debt of 8,240,700 specie dollars.

The Norwegian army, on a peace footing, numbers 12,-000 men; on a war footing, 18,000 men. The Landwehr is used exclusively for the defense of the country.

SWEDEN.

Sweden comprises an area of about 128,076 square miles, with a population of 4,160,677, and forms with Norway the whole of the peninsula known in ancient times by the name of Scandinavia.

The government of Sweden has at its head an hereditary constitutional sovereign, who possesses the sole executive, but shares the legislative power with the Diet or Parliament, composed of four chambers—1st, Nobility; 2d, Clergy; 3d, Burghers; and 4th, Peasants; which meet and vote separately.

PROVINCES.—Gottland; Sweden Proper; Norrland.

In the Swedish budget of 1868, the revenue is estimated at 36,461,270 rix-dollars; and the public debt, in 1865, was 74,068,000 rix-dollars.

The Swedish army, in 1868, consisted of 124,807 men; and the navy, of 17 armed steamers, carrying 132 guns, and 31 sailing vessels.

The present ruler of Norway and Sweden is King Charles XV., born May 3, 1826, and succeeded his father July 8, 1859.

TURKEY.

TURKEY comprises an area of 1,917,472 square miles, with a population of 40,000,000, distributed as follows:—

COUNTRIES.	Area.	Population.
Possessions in Europe	260,932	18,487,000
Possessions in Asia	667,326	16,463,000
Possessions in Africa	1,049,214	5,050,000
Total	1,977,472	40,000,000

The present Sultan is Abdul-Aziz-Khan, born February 9, 1830, and succeeded his brother June 25, 1857.

The Grand-Vizier is Midtul Pasha; and the Sheik-ul-Islam (chief of the Ulema, Judic, and Eulis—Supreme Council) is Hassan Effendi.

In 1868 the Sultan established a Council of State, which is divided into 5 departments—Administrative, Finance, Justice, Instruction, and Commerce—composed of 50 members, Christians and Mohammedans, elected by the Sultan; and a Supreme Court, consisting of 2 sections, civil and criminal.

The revenue (in 1866) consisted of 3,171,889 purses (purse, $24), and the public debt, of £69,142,270 sterling.

THE ARMY.

Nizam (regular army) consists of 130,496 men, divided into 6 corps (of which 30,000 men are in Crete, Tripoli, etc.).

Redif (reserve), 100,496; auxiliary troops of semi-independent provinces, states, etc., not subject to Nizam, 100,000; and irregular troops (Bashi-Bazouk, Tartars, etc.), about 90,000; making an aggregate available force in time of war, of over 420,000 men, and probably still greater increase.

The navy, in 1867, was composed of 185 war vessels, with 2,370 cannon, 18 of which were iron-clads having 498 guns.

The states which pay annual tribute to Turkey are:—

I. Egypt—Viceroy, Ismail Pacha, born November 6, 1816; became ruler in 1866, with title of Khedivi-el-Masr.

II. Principalities of Moldavia and Wallachia of Roumania—Hospodar, Prince Charles of Hohenzollern-Sigmaringen; elected April 20, 1866, and recognized by Turkey.

III. Servia—Prince Milan IV. (not of age); regency,

P. Blasnovar, J. Ristic, and J. Gavrianovic, of which Zemtich is President.

IV. Montenegro—Prince Nicholas I.; born 1840, and proclaimed in 1860.

The Council of State (Shurai Develet), as before reverted to, was introduced by the Sultan, May 11, 1868.

A GLIMPSE IN THE FUTURE.

MOTIVES AND PROBABILITIES OF THE WAR.

THE actual political condition of both France and Prussia is the partial realization of schemes that, like the famous Peter the Great policy of Russia, are traditional. United Germany has been the dream of Germans since Maria Theresa and the Great Frederick fought for supremacy. The contention was whether it should be Protestant or Catholic. The Prussia of to-day has swept away forever the tradition of the Holy Roman Empire. And it was reserved for Bismarck to demonstrate the impossibility of a voluntary federation of independent petty sovereigns, and the practicability of a welding of these several minor powers round the solid core of one great state, which should give solidity and cohesion to the mass. The political tendency of the Teutonic mind is to personal loyalty. The feudal sentiment which by the ferment and change of nearly a century has been obliterated in the French nation, is still the prevailing idea in Germany. Success always justifies enterprise with the majority of mankind; but this common acceptance of the *fait accompli* is not the only motive for German admiration of Prussia. She has realized in German fashion the preconception of German grandeur; her adherents and supporters being the great masses of the German-speaking tribes; the dissidents being the sovereign princes and powers whose characters or personalities were of no weight with their countrymen. The French on their part, whatever their internal convulsions, have always retained under every form of government the idea of a great empire with natural boundaries—the Alps, the Pyrenees, the Ocean, and the Rhine. This, whether in the days of Francis, of Richelieu, Louis XIV., the Republic, or the Empire, has been the French idea. Geographically, it is reasonable; ethnically, the only obstacle is the Rheno-German provinces. The first Napoleon himself even favored the idea of German unity, and mediatized a great number of petty powers which split up Germany like the squares of a chess-board, without its equality or regularity. But he also would have maintained the Rhine boundary had not his own towering ambition and the force of circumstances been too powerful.

Nice and Savoy were annexed to France at the close of the Italian war. So much was gained toward the dream of a compact, geographically defined France. Belgium to the west, with its ports on the North Sea, and the Rhenish provinces on the north will perfect the circumscription, and the accomplishment of this scheme will complete the *idées Napoléoniennes*, the tearing to pieces of the treaties of 1815. The Luxemburg business was but an offshoot of this great design. This is the French map of Europe. Whoever can lay it out and maintain it will be the Frenchman for the French.

The Rhine, from Rotterdam to Cologne, runs through a flat country. From this point to the junction of the Moselle there begins a succession of landscapes of wonderful beauty and variety—hill and dale, undulating slopes and rich plats. From Coblenz to Maxan the Rhine describes an irregular shallow curve. Strike another curve between those two points, about forty miles wide at its broadest part, and the area inclosed is the Rheno-German provinces, or, as it is now called, Rheno-Prussia. This is the territory for which France longs. From Basel to Carlsruhe the Rhine is already a French frontier line. Thence to Cleves it is German on both sides. Without Belgium, indeed, the Rhine provinces, if assigned to France, would be militarily untenable, running as they do in a wedge shape between trans-Rhenal Prussia and Belgium.

The people of the Rheno-Prussian provinces are German by race and language, which would scarcely predispose them in favor of a new or foreign master. Alsace, the German-French province in the Upper Rhine of which Strasbourg is the capital, is already an example of the fusion that might take place. The Alsatians speak both French and German—or, more correctly, speak neither. But there is no ground for assuming that they are not loyal to France, or that they have any desire to be Germanized. In calculating the chances of success to either party in the present European struggle, it is well not to lose sight of a principle whose influence has been manifest in every political upheaval in Europe for the last century. That principle was proved and established amidst the tremendous whirlwind of the French Revolution, upsetting and unsettling as it did all the ideas upon which human governments were supposed to be firmly based. *The will of the people is the governing power.* Now there is scarcely a power in Europe, save, perhaps, that of Russia, which dare wage war unless assured of popular support. A government not sustained by popular sentiment is almost sure to go to the wall in the contest. Thus modern wars are either actually or nominally undertaken in the interest of the people.

In the present contest we have the spectacle of both nations enthusiastically united in support of their respective leaders. The one is inspired by the memories of the First Empire, when the tri-color of France was carried victoriously over all Europe, and by love of *la patrie et la gloire.*

On the other hand, Prussia has rallied all Germany to her standard; while the great Germanic race throughout the world is dazzled by the almost realized vision of German unity.

UNITED STATES NAVY.

Our ships afloat are distributed as follows:—

THE NORTH ATLANTIC FLEET,

Or home squadron, consists of the Severn, second rate, flagship, 15 guns; the monitor Dictator, third rate, 2 guns; the double-turreted monitor Terror, third rate, 4 guns; Tuscarora, third rate, 6 guns; monitor Saugus, third rate, 2 guns; Swatara, fourth rate, 7 guns; Nantasket, fourth rate, 7 guns. Total—7 vessels, 43 guns.

SOUTH ATLANTIC FLEET.

Lancaster, first rate, flagship, 22 guns; Portsmouth, third rate, sailing sloop, 15 guns, and the Wasp, fourth rate, 1 gun. Total—3 vessels, 38 guns.

MEDITERRANEAN FLEET.

Franklin, first rate, flagship, 39 guns; Plymouth, second rate, 12 guns; Richmond, second rate, 18 guns; Juniata, third rate, 8 guns. Total—4 ships, 77 guns.

PACIFIC FLEET.

Saranac, second rate, flagship, 11 guns; Mohican, third rate, 6 guns; Kearsarge, third rate, 6 guns; St. Mary's, sailing sloop, third rate, 16 guns; Jamestown, third rate, sailing sloop, 16 guns; Onward, third rate, sailing sloop, 3 guns; Resaca, third rate, 7 guns; Cyanne, fourth rate, sailing sloop, 14 guns; Saginaw, fourth rate, 2 guns; Nyack, fourth rate, 3 guns; Ossipee, third rate, 9 guns. Total—11 ships, 93 guns.

ASIATIC FLEET.

Delaware, first rate, flagship, 21 guns; Ashuelot, third rate, 6 guns; Monocacy, third rate, 6 guns; Idaho, third rate, 7 guns. The Colorado, first rate, 46 guns, is *en route* to the East to relieve the Delaware, and the Benicia, third rate, 12 guns, and Alaska, third rate, 12 guns, are also on their way to this squadron. Total—7 ships, 110 guns.

ON SPECIAL SERVICE.

Michigan (Lake Erie), fourth rate, no guns given; Tallapoosa, third rate, dispatch boat; Yantic, fourth rate, 3 guns; Sabine, sailing frigate, second rate, 36 guns; Nipsic, fourth rate, 3 guns, Fishing Banks; Gerard, store ship, fourth rate, 4 guns, Fishing Banks; Frolic, fourth rate, 5 guns, Fishing Banks. Total—7 ships, 51 guns. Grand Total—30 ships, 412 guns.

The last Congress cut down the allowance of men to 8,500.

The following are the vessels at the various yards:

AT THE PORTSMOUTH (N. H.) YARD.

The corvette California, second rate, 2,400 tons, and carrying 21 guns, flag-ship of the Asiatic squadron. The sloop Narraganset, 566 tons, 5 guns. The Wyoming, 726 tons, 6 guns.

AT THE BOSTON NAVY YARD.

The frigate Wabash, 3,000 tons, 46 guns, one of the finest ships afloat; the corvette Shenandoah, 929 tons, 10 guns. The Worcester, a new ship of the second rate, 2,000 tons, and armed with 15 guns of heavy caliber. The corvette Ticonderoga, 1,019 tons, third rate, and carrying a splendid battery of 10 guns. The famous old frigate Niagara, 2,958 tons, 12 guns.

AT THE BROOKLYN YARD.

The Tennessee, formerly the Madawasca, has been greatly altered. She rates second, is 2,135 tons burden, and carries a battery of 23 heavy guns. The Guerriere, second rate, 2,490 tons, 21 guns; frigate Minnesota, 3,000 tons, 46 guns; Canandaigua, third rate, 955 tons, 10 guns; Saratoga, sailing sloop, third rate, 757 tons, 15 guns; Monongahela, third rate, 960 tons, 10 guns; corvette Albany, second rate, 2,000 tons, 15 guns; corvette Wachusett, third rate, 695 tons, 6 guns; Hartford, second rate, 2,000 tons, 18 guns.

PHILADELPHIA YARD.

The sloop Brooklyn, second rate, 2,000 tons, 20 guns. A light spar deck has been added to her. The Iroquois, third rate, 695 tons, 6 guns.

AT THE WASHINGTON YARD.

The Kansas, fourth rate, 410 tons, 3 guns, and at Norfolk, the Galena, fourth rate, 514 tons, 7 guns, and the Saco, fourth rate, 410 tons, 3 guns, are repairing. There are a number of other large ships at the various yards on the stocks.

NAVAL FORCE AT DISPOSAL.

The Navy Department could, on an emergency, place twenty-two additional ships at sea, carrying 267 guns of the average caliber. These added, would give us sixty-one cruisers, carrying a grand total of 725 guns, requiring 10,000 additional seamen.

The above is a clear *résumé* of our exact strength afloat, and at the various yards.

OUR IMPORTS AND EXPORTS TO GERMANY AND FRANCE.

The Extent of our Commercial Interest in the War.

GERMANY.

THE statistics contained in the following statements supply information which must prove of the highest interest by showing the extent to which our commerce will be interrupted if the Franco-Prussian conflict continues and the German ports are blockaded.

Our imports from the states in the Zollverein, which embraces nearly all Germany, for the fiscal year ending June 30, 1868, amounted to $21,569,988, and were received from the following states, in the quantities given:—

Imports to United States.

Prussia	$11,586,576
Saxony	5,660,384
Bavaria	1,897,314
Other German States	2,425,714
	$21,569,988

These imports were in the following quantities through the ports of countries named:—

England	$4,803,631
Bremen	10,243,934
Hamburg	4,876,220
France	170,248
Belgium	1,103,256
Holland	396,151
Not specified	6,498
	$21,569,988

The principal items in these imports are given in the following table:—

Books	$239,201	Calfskins, tanned	$323,078
Bristles	171,584	Skins tan'd, all upper leather	107,610
Buttons	289,757	Gloves	177,390
Analine	52,418	Musical instruments	272,326
Cotton Hosiery	2,522,232	Paintings	167,450
Laces	684,202	Writing paper	89,745
Cotton sundries	110,223	Paper sundries	125,350
Clothing	815,090	Pencils	104,066
Embroideries	146,298	Velvets	596,155
Beads	374,890	Ribbons	636,458
Pipes	101,778	Dress and piece goods	276,256
Toys	216,156	Silk	713,707
Dolls	126,614	Spirits and wines	421,656
Furs, undressed	146,553	Willow-ware	125,863
" dressed	410,323	Cloths	3,342,612
" hatters'	342,686	Woolen sundries	43,624
Glass	377,531	Shawls	60,560
Hops	333,696	Hosiery	134,953
Iron manufacture	68,710	Woolen and worsted goods	325,383
Penknives	133,326	Worsted sundries	164,891
General cutlery	75,432	Women's dress goods	851,127
Steel sundries	235,815	Webbing	653,555
Pig lead	546,046	Zinc	100,583

Our exports to Germany during the fiscal year ending June 30, 1869, amounted to $39,427,403 (including gold), and appear in the official returns as having been divided as follows:—

```
Prussia ...........................................$    949,138
Hamburg ..........................................  15,190,798
Bremen ...........................................  23,287,467
                                                   -----------
                                                   $39,427,403
```

Cotton, lard, petroleum, and tobacco are the chief products we sell to Germany; but as there is a large direct trade in these and other commodities transacted through the English markets, the figures below do not represent the full extent to which we find purchasers in Germany for our productions.

The following table gives the principal value of the products, agricultural and manufactures, we transport to Germany:—

	Hamburg.	Bremen.
Bark	$ 27,392	$ 24,180
Indian corn	45,211	13,734
Rye	224,260	268,971
Copper, pig, etc.	253,766	—
Cotton	1,792,947	11,835,231
Dyewoods	273,413	157,710
Furs	177,689	68,904
Gold bullion	1,623,469	39,200
" coin	4,167,131	721,390
Silver bullion	3,007,033	—
" coin	248,934	—
Hides	76,260	55,199
Muskets and rifles	184,082	257,935
General machinery	129,984	8,493
Sewing Machines	377,006	—
Rosin and turpentine	156,097	246,423
Petroleum benzine	8,961	—
" crude	29,677	113,378
" refined	2,572,431	24,360
Beef	138,745	1,059,678
Lard	348,077	14,653
Tallow	91,400	108,954
Tobacco, manufactured	39,637	4,730,900
" unmanufactured	269,194	132,726
Whalebone	119,186	—

The number of vessels, and their tonnage, which cleared for German ports in the fiscal year ending June 30, 1868, was as follows:—

	Am'n vessels.	Tons.	For'gn vessels.	Tons.
To Prussia	2	806	42	11,707
Hamburg	3	1,894	96	144,842
Bremen	24	31,586	241	271,057
Total	29	34,286	379	427,606

The number of vessels, and their tonnage, entered during the same time, was as follows:—

	Am'n vessels.	Tons.	For'gn vessels.	Tons.
Prussia	—	—	2	834
Hamburg	—	—	97	165,888
Bremen	16	30,971	187	242,324
Total	16	30,971	286	409,046

FRANCE.

Our exports to France during the fiscal year ending June 30, 1868, amounted to $45,945,864; of which $43,386,384 was to Atlantic ports, and $2,559,480 to Mediterranean ports.

Our imports from France amounted to $26,821,951; of which $23,444,815 was to the Atlantic, and $3,477,136 to Mediterranean ports.

The tonnage was as follows:—

	ENTERED.		CLEARED.	
	Am. tonnage.	For. tonnage.	Am. tonnage.	For. tonnage.
France on Atlantic..	64,923	74,678	114,513	73,523
France on Medit'n..	11,563	9,158	25,648	4,086
Total..........	76,486	83,836	140,161	77,609

THE GREAT EUROPEAN CONFLICT.

FRANCO-PRUSSIAN WAR.

AND

A Review of the Balance of Europe.

BY

GEO. W. BIBLE.

NEW YORK:
BIBLE BROTHERS, 432 BROOME STREET.

BIBLE BROTHERS,
SUBSCRIPTION BOOK PUBLISHERS,
432 Broome Street,
NEW YORK.

Publishers of Youth's Illustrated Bible History, Great European Conflict—Franco-Prussian War, &c.,

WHICH WILL BE FOLLOWED BY A SUCCINCT

HISTORY OF THE WAR.
Illustrated with Battle Scenes, Principal Generals of both Armies, etc., etc.

New, Popular, and Standard Works, specially suited to sales through agents, brought out from time to time.

Good, live, active agents wanted. To such special inducements are offered.

Conversant with the wants of the public in the book line, and fully alive to the times, we publish no books but those of popular standard character; the demand for which being already created, agents consequently make quick sales and large profits with little trouble.

SEND FOR CIRCULARS.

SOLD ONLY BY SUBSCRIPTION.

AGENTS WANTED FOR THE

YOUTH'S ILLUSTRATED
BIBLE HISTORY,

Embracing Distinguished Characters, Remarkable Events, Institutions, Manners, Customs, Natural History, Arts, Sciences, etc., etc., of

BIBLE LANDS AND TIMES.

By D. W. THOMPSON, A. M.,

MISSIONARY TO PALESTINE, AND LECTURER ON THE HOLY LAND.

TO WHICH IS ADDED A

Complete Chronological History of Events from the Creation of the World to the Completion of the Canon of the New Testament.

By JOHN BLAIR, LL. D.

Elegantly Embellished with nearly Three Hundred Engravings.

Making one of the most Instructive, Entertaining, and Elevating of all Books for Young People as well as those of more mature years.

The object of this work is to inspire youth with a love for the sacred volume, and draw their minds to its perusal and study, not as a stern and solemn duty, but as a delightful privilege. There is an absorbing interest attached to Scripture localities and Scripture times. If Troy and Thebes—if Athens and Rome are now visited with classic enthusiasm, how much more worthy of awakening the strongest emotions must be the country whose history as far transcends in interest that of every other, as its literature excels in sublimity all the ethics, and philosophy, and poetry, and eloquence of the heathen world.

This work places before the reader in a truthful, plain, but intensely interesting manner, all the important events, scenes, scenery, and incidents of the lands and places of the countries described in the Bible.

In producing the YOUTH'S BIBLE HISTORY, it has been the aim to make it a book universally acceptable to all denominations.

The engravings introduced will not only serve to illustrate, but will have the effect to *cultivate the mind—chasten the imagination—develop taste, and improve the heart.* Their importance as a great engine (if rightly applied) on the mind and heart, in aid of religion, government, moral and social order, and the well-being and happiness of the human race, is incalculable. To wean man from vice—win him to virtue, elevate him in the scale of being, or arouse him to deeds of valor, patriotism, or self-devotion, art becomes the proud ally of history and poetry, and takes its lofty station among the noblest productions of the human intellect; for the good of mankind, the honor of their country, and the glory of God.

The Land of Palestine abounds in scenes of the most picturesque beauty. Syria comprehends the snowy heights of Lebanon, and the majestic ruins of Tadmor and Baalbec. The gigantic temples of Egypt, the desolate plains of Babylon and Nineveh, the ancient cities of Idumea, Moab and Ammon, and the rocky solitudes of Mount Sinai, all afford subjects most admirably adapted to the artist's pencil.

THE CHRONOLOGICAL HISTORY forms a very important and indispensable feature in the completion of the work, and can not be too highly estimated. Although in condensed form, yet it furnishes a complete, comprehensive, and connected history of every important event from the creation of the World to the close of New Testament times. By the study of this Chronology one can soon become familiar with the whole history of the events portrayed in the Holy Bible, the Book of Books.

The price of the work is offered so low as to place it within the reach of every possessor of the Bible; and it is sincerely hoped that in addition to its claims as a pictorial family publication it may prove in a high degree *entertaining* and *useful*, and gladden many a fireside circle.

PRICE:

Beautifully Bound in Extra Cloth,...	$3.75
" " Embossed Leather	4.25
Handsomely Bound in Morocco Cloth, full gilt, beveled covers.	5.25
Elegantly Bound in Morocco, full gilt, beveled covers.........	7.50

Extra liberal inducements to good live agents.

SEND FOR CIRCULAR, TERMS, ETC.

Address—

BIBLE BROTHERS, Publishers,

432 Broome Street, New York.

www.ingramcontent.com/pod-product-compliance
Lightning Source LLC
Chambersburg PA
CBHW020253170426
43202CB00008B/355